*Introduction to a
Theological Theory of Language*

by the same author

LUTHER
THE NATURE OF FAITH
THEOLOGY AND PROCLAMATION
THE WORD OF GOD AND TRADITION

Introduction
to a Theological
Theory of Language

GERHARD EBELING

Translated by R. A. Wilson

Collins

ST JAMES'S PLACE, LONDON

1973

William Collins Sons & Co Ltd
London · Glasgow · Sydney · Auckland
Toronto · Johannesburg

First published by J. C. B. Mohr (Paul Siebeck),
Tübingen, 1971, as *Einführung in Theologische Sprachlehre*
© Gerhard Ebeling
J. C. B. Mohr (Paul Siebeck) Tübingen 1971
© in the English translation
William Collins Sons & Co Ltd, London,
and Fortress Press, Philadelphia, 1973
ISBN 0 00 215345 9
Set in Monotype Bembo
Made and Printed in Great Britain by
William Collins Sons & Co Ltd, Glasgow

Contents

Contents

CONTENTS

A Letter in Place of a Preface

. . . I vividly remember your attendance at my lectures during
the summer term of 1970. It often happens when I am
lecturing – and preaching as well – that a certain face stands
out and attracts my glance. Perhaps it is because this face looks
particularly critical or expectant. I sometimes feel then as
though I were speaking mainly to this one person. And in the
thoughts which accompany what I am saying there may even
spring up something of an argument with him. Quite often this
impression persists later when I am at my desk preparing the
next lecture, and affects the ideas and the way they are formulated, although of course not to any measurable degree. The
next time I involuntarily keep an eye open, with some trepida-
tion, for this silent partner in the dialogue, and I am rather
sad if he is not there. You very rarely disappointed me in this
way. Thus your attendance at the lectures was closely linked
for me with the course they took. So I am very pleased to
send you this printed version.

In its basic features it varies little from the spoken form. But
much in it will appear new to you. After making many correc-
tions on the draft which I used for the actual lectures, I worked
over the fair copy made from it so thoroughly that on many
pages there was not a single line unaltered. I mention this only
because I would like to take this opportunity of saying something to you concerning the practice of giving lectures, about
which there is so much dispute nowadays. You will be aware
of the slogans which are used to criticize, if not to ridicule it.
I shall not deal with them in detail. I have almost twenty-five

years of experience of preparing new lectures – only in rare and exceptional cases have I re-used an old manuscript – and the educational results have often been terribly small, as the examinations revealed. So I really have no illusions about it. The necessity for reforms in this respect is obvious. But such reforms are in line with the educational aims of the university only if they assist in achieving a meaningful use of lectures, and an ability to make use of them in a reasonable way.

I must admit that I would never finish a book of this kind if the stimulus – and often enough the compulsion – provided by the lectures and the expectant audience did not impel me to work it out step by step. It seems at first sight a very sensible suggestion that at the beginning of the term lecturers should hand out copies of their notes, and instead of treating the students to a monologue, should hold discussions with them. But it is a suggestion based on a very innocent view of how a course of lectures is composed. Of course adequate opportunity must be given for discussion. And of course circumstances vary, both in respect of the object of the lectures and the way different lecturers teach. But if it is a question of allowing others to share in an independent process of research and thought, one cannot just assume that the whole thing can be taken out of a drawer at the beginning of term. And this would really be against the proper interests of the students. By their reactions, questions and suggestions they ought to play some part in determining the style and content of lectures, and in this way to exercise the responsibility they share for the process of teaching and learning. And there is a quite common type of lecturer, who, not for reasons of laziness or under the pressure of preparing his first course of lectures, but all his life, lives from hand to mouth and never finishes his preparation until it is time to set out for the lecture room. There are obvious disadvantages in this but there is also something to be said for it.

Students are fairly often sympathetic to this approach.

Here I must mention another point. This course of lectures was given the pretentious title 'A Theological Theory of Language'. When I choose a theme for a course of lectures, I prefer one that I am sure no one will come to hear just for the sake of his examinations. And this was not the first time that I have taken on something which has forced me, by the very fact that I have given notice of it, to apply myself to a necessary task, even if it was beyond my own capabilities. That the experiment made me more modest, you will be able to tell from the strong note of reservation which I have since added to the title. But a course of lectures is also valuable from this point of view. It permits experiment. One can make statements which, from an academic point of view, remain provisional. And yet to give one's ideas a well-prepared spoken form calls for a high degree of exact exposition, much more than is normally necessary in a more or less extempore utterance. When one is attempting something risky, this requirement, and the ability to experiment, often combine to produce something for which under other circumstances one would usually lack the courage and productive energy.

This may sound terribly much as though lectures had an educational value for lecturers, but not for students. If one removes the exclusive note from the positive part of this statement, there is some truth in it. How far the negative part can be refuted, I should like to state in principle, ignoring all detailed problems, by a personal experience. In my first term as a student I followed a course of lectures by Rudolf Bultmann on the subject 'Theological Encyclopaedia',* although he tried to dissuade first-degree students from attending. I did not understand a great deal of it, but in spite of this, or perhaps even because it was so demanding, it decisively motivated my theological studies, and left an ineffaceable impression of

*The academic discipline which treats of individual branches of theological study as component parts of the whole of theology. (Trans.)

academic excellence. So I am convinced that a course of lectures which asks rather too much of students, not just by the level of argument, but also by the general difficulty of assimilating what is said, can provide a stimulus which is not without value. This is all the more so if the lecture is available afterwards in an authentic form for careful discussion. In addition, their previous encounter with the material as delivered orally can actually be a considerable help in understanding the printed version, an advantage which someone who has heard the lectures possesses over the mere reader.

As you will realize, these considerations have a connection with my concern in undertaking a theological theory of language. Perhaps all that remains of the total impression you gained is that the problems of theology are interwoven in a characteristic way with those of language and understanding. From time to time you may well have thought that you were not attending a lecture in the faculty of theology at all, until suddenly the theological theme returned, particularly in the context of the various observations about living experience. I would be fortunate if I were not completely wrong in thinking that this struck you as the basic note of the course. All the same, I am conscious that this may have aroused expectations in you which this mere introduction unfortunately cannot fulfil.

As I have already mentioned, I have not altered the basic features of the lectures. If I had tried to comment even to a modest degree upon the various different approaches to the understanding of language, to deal with the literature, to discuss at length the problems of fundamental theology which were constantly raised, to expound at greater length the statements which towards the end of the book became more and more concentrated, and throughout the lectures to work out the relationship to experience in a more lively and concrete fashion, I would have had to start again at the beginning in a different way. I have contented myself with what I was capable of at the moment, disregarding all the further tasks required. This was to prepare the way for others to think the matter out for themselves; and this seemed worth while. How much or how little I have learnt from others to this end may be judged by the specialists into whose field of competence I have often strayed. I have almost entirely refrained from giving the usual apparatus of notes and indexes. This work is intended to be neither a learned monograph nor a compendium of knowledge, nor even the manifesto of a new programme for theology. Rather, I have restricted myself to the style of a meditation. If anyone were to assign the book to theological devotional literature, I should not regard this as the condemnation which such a judgment might be presumed to imply. For reading a book of this kind requires a reader who allows himself time to think over the matter for himself and is not trying to read the book through at a sitting. Perhaps even many non-theological readers are more willing to do this, and will not take offence at a number of specialist theological terms which could scarcely be avoided, nor even a number of what appear to be theological bad habits, and which may possibly have been avoidable, but which are difficult to set aside.

As you take up again what you heard in the lecture room, you may be more provoked to disagreement than you were then. But I would like to hope that you might cling all the more firmly – more firmly than I succeeded in doing – to the view that the mystery of reality and the mystery of language form an inseparable unity which we always encounter together. To this end may I give you these lines by Hölderlin to go with you: 'Oh that my heart may never grow older, that none of the joys, the thoughts of men, the tokens of life may be despised by me . . .; for all these the heart needs to speak unutterable things.'

Yours,

17 February 1971   GERHARD EBELING

13

Preliminary Note

It would be understandable, and in some respects a very healthy reaction, if the undertaking of a theological theory of language were to be regarded as not particularly attractive and were even to provoke profound mistrust. We do well to call to mind the possible causes of disquiet, the difficulties and the resistance which we must expect. If we share some of these doubts ourselves, we must formulate them, so that they are no longer mere vague impressions, but are given clear, though provisional, expression. And in so doing we must also to some extent submit them to criticism. There may be some for whom all this has long meant little or nothing, either because they have uncritically followed a school of thought in which the term 'theory of language' has already become fashionable jargon, or because they do not look for anything of use at all from this phrase. It is they who will profit most from the stimulus to further thought which a few questions will provide.

I begin by classifying the mass of problems which arise into three groups, entitled: 'Boredom with Language', 'The Jungle of the Problem of Language', and 'Scepticism about a Mere Theory of Language'. In the fourth section I then go on to discuss the basic questions of a theological theory of language. But in so classifying my material I do not claim to have dealt with the problems at all fully or in proper systematic form.

Boredom with Language

Boredom with language, boredom with words. This tells us
in a phrase what the present crisis of Christianity consists of,
and where its deepest roots lie. For Christian faith, above all
in its Reformation form, the word is an essential element; and
yet confidence in it has largely disappeared. Dialectical theology consciously returned to the Reformation inheritance
and proclaimed itself a theology of the word. At the present
day, by contrast, there is an almost allergic reaction to the
mention of the word of God. The idea is attractive, but is
felt to be empty of content. It is seen as a kind of magic
formula, as an ideology or a mere turn of phrase. To make
anything of it in a responsible fashion seems beyond our
capabilities. Of course on the level of theological debate such
blunt statements are not usually made. But there are theologians
who feel obliged to set about their task by contrasting the reality
of revelation as *history* with the primacy of the word; or else
they make the Utopian *hope*, which gives imaginative force
and stimulus to revolutionary action, compete with the
primacy of *faith*, which clings to the word. There are certain
elements of truth in this and other similar new starting points
in theology. They are worth noticing as alarm signals, whenever a preoccupation with the basic Reformation formula
'word and faith' turns into the narrow and rigid outlook to
which terms such as literalism and fideism are applicable,
and which can be condemned as a flight into inward life and
an individualistic understanding of salvation.

Of course the 'theology of the word' was itself a reaction

against pious subjectivism. But its adoption of the concept of the word as its watchword, in polemic opposition to the phenomenon of experience, was always somewhat questionable and did not accurately represent what actually took place in the theological revolution after the First World War. The beginnings of dialectical theology were determined very much by experience! The passionate rejection of the nineteenth century was determined more by certain psychological needs and blind spots deriving from the clash between two generations than from a clear understanding of the pattern of the history of theology. There was a failure to recognize that, for example, the concept of the inner life in Wilhelm Herrmann, or the concept of absolute dependency in Schleiermacher, was only apparently and superficially in conflict with the new views. But these theologians were endeavouring to break down a concept of the word which was stunted and set in a mould of orthodox rigidity. They sought the word as it were in the condition of flowing lava – where the link between the word and life did not need to be restored retrospectively and with great trouble, but welled up with elemental force, as the springing up of the word in the processes of life and the issuing forth of life from a living and life-giving word. The fear of a loose and vitiated understanding of the spirit had taken such a hold that there was not the courage to integrate the word and the spirit, the word and life, and the word and experience in the right way.

The slogan 'boredom with words' takes us beyond such contemporary reminiscences to a very much wider historical context. We are not concerned merely with a temporary reaction to the way in which a theological concept has become worn out. For the 'theology of the word' itself arose from a deeply felt experience of the weakness and impotence of Christian language, from the temptation to boredom at the traditional language of the Church, and from a vigorous apprehension of the paradox of the word of God in human language, as an impossible possibility. This corresponds, in different circumstances, to the struggles of Schleiermacher or Wilhelm Herrmann against the orthodox, rationalist or purely traditionalist optimism of the word which was to blame for the runaway devaluation of Christian language and so for the loss of confidence in words. Here we are describing a situation with which the theology of modern times had to come to grips from the first. It represents a basic theme running through the whole of the recent history of theology: *Assent is no longer freely given to the tradition of Christian language.*

I. CHRISTIANITY AND CULTURE

What Christian faith calls the word of God is not, and never was, 'self-evident' to man (in the trivial and pejorative sense of the phrase). He was never able to take it in smoothly, without trouble and painlessly – and without joy, as this would no doubt have meant. Agreement with what was proclaimed and addressed to one never took place without difficulties, and assent was never automatic. The believer has always owed his faith to a miracle, to a radical change of mind which overwhelms him. According to Luther, the word of God always comes as *adversarius noster*, our adversary. It does not simply confirm and strengthen us in what we think we are and as what we wish to be taken for. It negates our nature, which has fallen prey to illusion; but this is the way the word of God affirms our being and makes it true. This is the way, the only way, in which the word draws us into concord and peace with God. This structure of the certainty of justification, which is none other than the belief in creation and the hope of the resurrection, is in a sense also the basic pattern of the miraculous power of the word of God. It is a power which one cannot grow used to, to which one cannot become indifferent, and which one cannot take under one's control; and the giving of assent to the testimony borne to it is itself experienced as a miracle. But all this, as it happens to the believer, is genuinely self-evident – in a stricter and more precise sense of the term. He does not give his assent to it because his heart is forced and broken, but because it is set free and made whole.

But in the history of Christianity the *miracle* of a word which is '*self-evident*' (in the strict sense of the word) was quickly transformed into a situation in which, as a *miracle*, it was *self-evident* in the trivial sense. Of course such a wholesale judgment oversimplifies matters. The truth and its perversion always coexist, closely entangled with each other, and do not simply follow each other like periods of history. But what do change from one period to another are the conditions of understanding, or, as we might also call them, certain basic features of the language situation.

For about fifteen hundred years the tradition of Christian language was fully and publicly accepted, and in consequence was also the determinative element in general education. The tradition of Christian language to which we refer here is a very complex entity. Of course it includes biblical language; it usually consists, however, neither of this alone, nor of this only in its original form, but of biblical language enriched with the borrowed and assimilated vocabularies of the ancient world and translated into the Koine of the traditional language of the Church. This idiom was mainly preserved through the medium of Latin, a circumstance which produced effects extending into the living vernaculars, and it was extraordinarily powerful and enduring. It created a wide area of mutual understanding and assent not only between contemporaries, but over many generations which were thus drawn together as contemporaries, speaking the same language, in a Christianized age.

The tradition of Christian language was as familiar to the people of that age as their mother tongue, because it was merged with it. It was coextensive with the intellectual environment in which people lived, and corresponded to a universal understanding of reality. It offered a world picture which took in the whole of the supraterrestrial and sub-terrestrial regions, a historical picture which extended over the whole of time from the creation to the end, and an under-standing of existence which had a place for everything in life, everything that fills life or leaves it empty from birth to death. And according to this understanding, this earthly life was surrounded, sustained, interpenetrated and overshadowed by eternal life. There existed nothing, and according to the basic underlying conception there could exist nothing, which was not already drawn into the orbit of the tradition of Christian language and had already been uttered in it.

This should not be taken to mean that the powerful sense of being familiar with and at home in the tradition of Christian language was bound of itself to bar the way to the essence of Christian faith. One must not overlook the extraordinarily valuable elements to be found in it. But the dangers are obvious. It was very easy for a miracle to be something which is self-evident in the trivial sense. This does not mean that the miracle of the word of God, and miracles in general, were no longer mentioned, but rather that what is said about them takes them far too much for granted. It was no longer easy to reach the point where true assent could replace merely inherited assent. Independent judgment and decision came to seem possible only as a refusal of assent, as nonconformity.

It took a long time for this situation to change. The first thing that happened was that dissent arose within the tradition of Christian language itself, and this destroyed the appearance which it gave of being self-evident. This process began with the great heretical movements of the height of the Middle

Ages, and it decisively changed the face of the age in the sixteenth century with the setting up of two different Christian dialects, if one may use such formal terms. Seen from a distance, the difference of language between the denominations does not seem so great, but in fact it conceals within itself barriers to agreement which have in fact not been overcome up to the present day. At any rate, Christianity found itself once again faced with the element of personal decision regarding its public language. But this movement in its turn immediately became frozen into a pattern which can actually be pinpointed geographically – even after centuries – and which represents a constant factor in the historical process down to the present day. Once more there took place a transition to an assent which had become something self-evident.

This finally began to be broken down by the tensions that arose between the tradition of Christian language and the scientific experience of the universe. The problems that have arisen as a result are unusually complicated. For all kinds of misunderstandings and possibilities of divergent judgment have been superimposed upon a situation which is complex in itself. This of course can be seen as a gain, in so far as the confusing intermingling of the language of faith and the language of the general experience of the world has been disentangled. As a result of this intermingling, both the language of faith and that of the experience of the world had lost their freedom. But their disentanglement only does what it ought, that is, sets free both sides, as long as it does not give the impression that there is no relationship between them. The same ambivalence, therefore, applies to the process of emancipation in which not only the natural sciences and technology, but also law and ethics, and all the humanities, have won freedom of language, so establishing the linguistic pluralism which is characteristic of the modern age. This process ought to have been to the benefit of the language of faith, but this has not always been so. The course of events has in part been painful and unfortunate, which shows how difficult it is to escape the conditions of an age which is coming to an end, and the language situation contained in it. Even where the basic realization has been made that the Bible and Church doctrine cannot and should not prejudice scientific knowledge, or attempt to impose a standard upon it, the process of disentanglement has not been without its problems in matters of detail. For it imposes a number of difficult tasks with regard to the language of faith. That language has been handed down in a form in which the content of faith has as it were been amalgamated with the general cultural situation of a particular age. But endeavours to resist the danger of a loss of contact with the tradition of Christian language, however well intentioned, are in fact liable to increase this danger. People have been made conscious of it, but it does not seem to have been overcome.

An example of this is the debate about demythologization. The obstinately persistent charge of elimination which is made against the programme of demythologization sees the threat to Christian faith in the sacrificing of certain parts of the tradition of Christian language to what is regarded as an arbitrary attempt at purification. Of course if an amputation of this kind were really taking place and if it extended to essentials, it would be dangerous. It may be claimed that statements are not being eliminated but merely interpreted, and that what has become incomprehensible is not being deleted, but only replaced by an appropriate and much clearer translation; but this of course does not guarantee what the actual result is. But whatever one's judgment of individual cases, the really disturbing problem seems to me to lie elsewhere.

For assent to be achieved to the tradition of Christian language, the mere deletion of certain elements is in some ways the easiest operation. It can on occasions present extraordinary difficulties, but it can also be a response to a genuine need.

Whatever the circumstances, this procedure has the advantage of being a clearly defined operation. And the outcome – or so at least it appears – is the possibility of complete assent, though perhaps only to a tradition of Christian language much reduced in content. But the same is not true of the process of interpretation. There can be no doubt that this task is both necessary and justified. The fundamentally primitive process of trimming our dialogue with the biblical text to what we can assent to directly and without any need of interpretation rests on an illusion and does violence to the text. The attempt to separate mechanically what is always valid from what has become invalid ignores the historical nature of every utterance, the way it is interwoven in the context of its time. If this is ignored, the biblical word itself is not taken seriously. And therefore the task of interpretation can never be replaced by a kind of sieve, with which it may be hoped to separate the religious wheat from the historical chaff.

But what is profoundly disturbing is not so much the question whether the task of interpretation can ever succeed, whether it is possible for texts from a distant age and a strange context to utter their message in a new age and a new context, whether the words frozen in a text can ever become living words again and give the power to say something relevant at the present day. The question, in short, whether the spirit preserved in the letter can once again become spirit *through* the letter, and yet in a certain sense *against* the letter, by creating the presence of the spirit (for spirit by its very nature has this power of making present). This question, I consider, is one which can straight away be answered in the affirmative, however wide-ranging and profound the problems may be which this affirmative answer imposes. The very least degree of interest in a book, in communication with what, at any moment, is the past, refutes the *a priori* doubt whether an understanding which transcends time, and which paves the way to assent, are possible at all. Language itself, impregnated with history, constant through history and yet changing with the course of history, refutes every objection to the mere possibility of interpretation. For language itself is ultimately nothing other than the power which creates understanding and brings people to understand each other.

What is disturbing is the question whether this fundamental and unquestioned affirmation of the possibility of interpretation in at least some sense, gives any guarantee that the tradition of Christian language in particular can survive in a changed era. Is it possible in this special case in fact to achieve an understanding which has the character of assent, that is, in which the hearer agrees with the statement on his own account? This question can be answered, in the affirmative or the negative, only in the process of interpretation itself. Assent or the refusal of assent can only take place in the course of honest endeavour to understand. We must not brush aside the difficulties on which we are touching here. Yet on principle we can subscribe to an answer to this question which is as assured an affirmative as ever; for there are signs, incontestably present even in our own time, that the tradition of Christian language is not only claiming but is finding the same interest as before. This statement says little enough, but it aims to say the minimum; and yet even to agree with this minimum is almost bound to take one further.

But even if one admits the possibility of assent to the tradition of Christian language, and even if many testify that it has been achieved, the question remains, under what conditions and at what cost this has come about! To a disturbing degree it seems to involve educational requirements which can hardly be reconciled with the universal c'aim of Christian faith. Can something which is a matter of life and death and concerns all men, be tied to certain educational conditions without being contradictory in itself?

The powerful implications of so radical a posing of the question should not prevent us from patiently appreciating the many aspects of the whole matter. In Christianity there has always – with relatively few shameful exceptions – been an extraordinarily close link between faith and education. An impressive list of examples can be brought forward to demonstrate this. Anyone who becomes a Christian has to assimilate a certain amount of knowledge. He has to learn (and this includes a reasonable amount of learning by heart). He is expected to be able to give an account of his faith. He is assumed to be capable of the achievement, by no means to be despised, of following a sermon attentively. His whole thought and behaviour are meant to be determined by an education of the heart. All this indicates that the miracle of becoming a Christian, as we have described it, is utterly remote from magic or hypnosis, as much as faith is distinct from superstition.

Wherever Christianity establishes itself, it sets up schools which not only teach religion but also, as their main work, teach general subjects and undertake the task of education. Moreover, from the very earliest times Christianity has given a training in theology, to a degree which is not found in any other religion. In this training, the knowledge of languages, the study of history, philosophy and the relation of theology to other branches of knowledge have always been regarded as of such importance that if the study of theology ever remains true to what it intrinsically demands it can be described without exaggeration as the most demanding and universal study of all. But for the same reason it tends to demand too much of the student and to bog him down in an education which is only half complete.

The history of the Church, then, constantly reveals the tensions of mistrust and overpresumption in the relationship between the simple believer and the theological expert. There is nothing new in this, in the fact that such labels can mean different things and are deceptive. Simplicity can be stupidity in disguise. Theological expertise can sometimes turn into narrow-minded and incomprehending specialism. And what is represented as the responsibility of the clergy must not necessarily be interpreted on the model of the Grand Inquisitor. But in spite of all distortions and signs of malaise Christianity has always endeavoured to avoid being something which is only for the simple, or only for those who have an education in the narrower sense. It has always tried to demonstrate its good will towards education by being extensive enough to include all levels of education.

An infinite number of examples of the complex subject of 'Christianity and culture' could be given, and each one would be subject to critical reservations. But our argument is principally concerned with the following. During the Christianized era, when there was large-scale intermingling of the tradition of Christian language and general education, to learn and adopt the tradition of Christian language was a much more straightforward and universal part of education. In a single process of learning and living people learned to understand the language of Christian faith and to speak it themselves, and so to make direct use of it. It was much as if they were learning their mother tongue, with which a person unconsciously grows familiar through the elementary and unified experience of learning to speak at all. There is of course some question whether, in a period when Latin was the language of public worship and theology, Christianity was not threatened by being conducted in a foreign tongue, and whether a dangerous linguistic dichotomy, between personal piety in the vernacular, and true Christian education in the ecclesiastical and learned language, was not at the very least being institutionalized. The linguistic dichotomy which we find there was certainly questionable, but in its structure was basically different from the linguistic dichotomy which the Christian at the present day is expected to submit to and to overcome.

Because of the breach between the tradition of Christian language and general education, the task of learning and adopting the former inevitably has the character of a conscious process of education. Since the language of Christian faith derives from a different educational situation from that of the present day, it necessarily carries something of the air of a foreign language, even in a vernacular version. To make personal use of it demands in every case some degree of historical consciousness. It is too simple to say that the education of our own age has in any case taken on historical features, and that therefore an historical attitude to the tradition of Christian language is inevitable for present-day man. The reverse is the case. The fact that Christian faith is to an unusual degree rooted in history stimulated an awareness of history, the moment the tradition of Christian language and general education diverged. I have no wish to be the advocate of a violently one-sided thesis. Many factors are unquestionably involved here. But the conflict between the force represented by present-day education, and that represented by tradition, which is by no means spent, is fundamental to an attitude to history which is in essence no longer based on assent to a history handed down by tradition, but rather looks critically at the self-perpetuating historical tradition and is emancipated from the authority of tradition. But Christian faith, even in the modern age, has maintained an absorbing interest in this particular tradition of language. And the weight of this tradition has made the tension with the emancipated world of modern education particularly acute. But without this interest and without this tension, the modern awareness of history, with the contradictory demand it makes on history – to be enriched by it and at the same time to be set free from it – would not have been so virulent.

Does the educational situation of the modern age require a Christian, in his relationship to the origin and source of faith, to bypass the modern awareness of history, in so far as he cannot do without the mediation of the tradition of Christian language? The answer seems to be clear: Of course not! In so far as Christian faith is created historically, this mediation must be reflected upon historically. This need not cause any harm. On the contrary, the twofold movement of historical thought as it contemplates its subject from outside – on the one hand an estrangement from tradition and on the other hand an interpretation which endeavours to understand it and to test the possibility of assent – can in fact purify the relationship to tradition. For it guards against the danger of calling for assent at the wrong point and obtaining it by deceit or causing it to be prematurely declared impossible. Here we have described, in extremely schematic terms, the task which is faced by theology in the educational situation of the modern age. To forestall the misunderstandings which might arise from this abbreviated formula, we must explicitly emphasize that if an interpretation which endeavours to understand seriously desires to test the possibility of assent, it must come to terms with the whole complexity of the present-day experience of the world. For true assent cannot come about if artificial limits are placed on the confrontation which takes place within it.

The question of the relationship to the tradition of Christian language in the educational situation of the modern age has shown us the task of theology. But we are not concerned in the first instance with the way in which theologians in the modern age have approached this hermeneutic task. Rather, we shall ask what are the consequences of the changed language situation for Christianity, for the Church and the individual believer. If it is true that to become familiar with and to adopt the tradition of Christian language is something which now has the character of a conscious educational process, then faith seems to be associated with conditions which simply cannot be fulfilled, unless it can largely be left separate from the business of adapting the tradition of Christian language. The dilemma which presents itself here is exemplified in the contradictory tendencies which in the modern age have determined the relationship between faith and theology.

On the one hand, a basic insight into the situation of the Christian in the modern age was displayed by Semler, and after him by Schleiermacher and many others. They strongly emphasized the distinction between religion (or devotion or faith as the case may be) and theology. To have religion is something different from the possession of a knowledge of religious things. Faith must not be confused with the theological learning concerning matters of faith. These assertions are directed against the orthodox understanding in which the knowledge of the objects of faith plays a dominant role. The list of articles of faith which it is necessary to salvation to know becomes so long that a considerable degree of theological knowledge must be attributed to the individual believer. In accordance with this, the word 'theology' in orthodox Christian thinking was always largely understood in the sense of 'the knowledge of God' in general, so that the boundaries between the knowledge of faith and theology were fluid. Since the eighteenth century, however, the use of the word 'theology' has been limited strictly to a specialist branch of knowledge, and has been clearly distinguished from the concerns of religious devotion and of each individual believer. But this does not merely represent a rejection of the orthodox understanding. Another factor at work is that as a result of a changed intellectual situation, theology itself took on more and more the character of a specialized branch of knowledge, particularly in the form of historical theology. It would have been absurd to burden the believer as such with this academic material. In addition, theology as an academic study is concerned in general not merely with knowledge, but with the development of an awareness of the problems and with showing the way to attain to methodical and critical understanding on one's own responsibility. If only because of the talents and time this requires, it is not something of which everyone is capable. It is something to be left to specialists.

But the result of this has necessarily been that the importance of this academic theology for the act of faith is itself reduced. For a faith that had to wait for the results would have to wait a long time, unless it were to acquiesce in a single briefly held and rapidly revised scholarly opinion – and if so, which? For faith to be dependent on the vagaries of academic theology is too obviously nonsensical for us to spend any longer describing the consequences. The average clergyman in fact settles for the theology which he has encountered while a student and within which, with all the accidental features that occur in it, he has made his choice. For the layman, it is even more the case that in matters of theology his information runs to a very limited and fortuitous selection of theological knowledge, coarsened and distorted by unavoidable simplification. At this level inner insecurities lead to theological tendencies becoming more fossilized than ever. But it is contradictory to the nature of faith for people, for the sake of faith, to hand themselves over blindly to human authority and to renounce their personal conviction and their own responsibility, and indeed to dress up as an authority something which of its nature cannot be and does not wish to be an authority. For academic knowledge is always obliged to make the reservation that a better understanding may be achieved. Because it is concerned with objective certainty, it does not allow itself to claim an absolute and definitive personal certainty. It does not seek to be believed, but to be checked and critically examined.

This instructive argument, which asserts and explains the profound gulf between faith and theology in the modern age, can be complemented by one which runs in precisely the opposite direction. Never in the whole of the history of the Church has faith been so dependent upon conscious theological study as in the modern age. Of course the Christian has had to be ready at any time to make a defence to anyone who calls him to account for the hope that is in him.[1] This is not for the sake of a missionary activism, which is in addition to his faith, but for the sake of faith itself. For faith is not blind and dumb. Something has been revealed to faith, it has learned something, and so is able to speak, and in particular to give an account of its own basis and consequences. Faith is given and experienced in words. Because it lives by the words it receives, so its life extends to the words by which it vindicates itself. Its life would be strangled if it were condemned to speechlessness. The way in which this structural feature of Christian faith develops varies greatly with changing historical circumstances. It would be extremely instructive to write a church history from the point of view of whether Christians at various periods were enabled or made unable, whether they succeeded or failed, to make a defence of their faith, or, in other words, to vindicate their Christianity in terms of language.

It would be particularly revealing to study this connection between Christians and the language they had at their disposal in the earliest period of church history. For this was a time when theology was first taking shape, and changed and fluctuated to an extraordinary degree. No formal dogma yet claimed to prescribe the grammar of orthodoxy. The pattern of public life and thought was determined by traditions quite different from that of Christianity. Faith had to be expressed in a non-Christian environment and defence of it had to be made by individuals, depending on their own resources, to other members of the family, neighbours and the authorities.

So far as one can penetrate this layer of church history at all, largely lost as it is in anonymity, many interesting facts are revealed by these early stages. There are factors in the elementary language of faith which it is easy for us to overlook, because we are accustomed to a mature and structured ecclesiastical language and theology. These factors include the legitimate power of the language of symbols and gestures – for example the sign of the cross, the early Christian symbol of the fish or the kiss of peace. All these are expressions of an intrinsic 'pregnancy' in the literal sense, a speech pregnant and full of meaning, containing and offering much more than it makes explicit. We still undergo something like the same experience in the language of love. Or one may mention the powerful statement made by certain kinds of behaviour, by acts and forms of life which in an eloquent and convincing way establish and maintain fellowship. It is probable that in the very earliest days of the Church such elements took on great importance, for the identification of Christianity as something distinct, and for the precise definition of what a Christian has to say to the world. One recalls the charitable work, the attitude to women, the treatment of social divisions as no more than relative, the simplicity of liturgical forms, the acceptance of martyrdom, etc. Finally one must note what might be called the mystery of the present moment: the *kairos* of a gospel, the language of which touches on reality so directly in a particular situation that merely to utter it brings a participation in its powerful force.

We have already shown how unconsciously an individual Christian would accept and adopt the tradition of Christian language in the Christianized era. This made it possible for even the simplest person to give verbal expression to his faith. In the atmosphere of a general assent which was already present and could be assumed, it was possible for anyone to rely confidently and without assertion on this language, the validity of which was uncontested, and delegate responsibility for it to the Church and to theology.

Of course the interest of the laity in theological questions, which began when the Middle Ages were at their height, is a sign within the Christianized era of the first modest steps towards the maturity of the Christian. It is clear that its roots lay on the one hand in the need, arising from faith itself, for a continuous growth towards maturity and independence, and on the other hand in the increasing education of the laity, and in particular of the rising middle class, which again brought with it changes in the way the individual believer regarded himself. But even under the influence of humanism and the Reformation, with their criticism of the church hierarchy and scholastic theology – all of which met with a lively response from the laity in particular – the total and direct immersion in the tradition of Christian language was by no means replaced by a conscious attitude towards it.

But in the modern period this became increasingly the case. The question now is not whether the conscious attitude of an outsider towards the tradition of Christian language is a danger to faith or cannot be reconciled to it. We dealt briefly with this objection when we discussed the possibility of interpretation. The question that now arises is rather whether the degree of conscious study required is not in practice, for most people, a hindrance to faith. The traditional language of Christian faith needs to be interpreted because – taken as a whole – it can no longer be directly adopted as our own. Not that it is possible to replace it by another, which would remove the necessity for interpretation. For the aim of interpretation is in fact to achieve a relationship of familiarity to the interpreted language, to use it in the right way. It seeks, for example, to liberate biblical words such as 'heaven', 'resurrection' or 'sin' from the misunderstandings to which they inevitably lead if they are understood in an unconsidered way at the present day. Precisely such an unconsidered understanding would result in a falsifying modernization. This would happen either if it led to an acceptance of Christian faith in the form of a positivism of revelation or a rejection of it in the form of a positivism of science. By contrast, an interpretation which takes into account the differences of language that exist endeavours not to do violence to the traditional language but to allow what is contained in it to be effective in the present-day context.

It seems that we are being led here into a hopeless impasse. Most people will not acknowledge the challenge of such an attitude of conscious and reflective interpretation to the tradition of Christian language. They are not capable of the effort of making the double movement, standing aside from the tradition to examine it historically and then returning to it to interpret and recover it. They do not even see the necessity for this expenditure of energy. And even if their intellectual abilities and firm intent permit, they lack the time required to deal honestly with the problem. The consequences are catastrophic. Even those who want to be Christians and profess themselves such are seized with a profound uncertainty about the language of faith. They no longer know how to use the traditional Christian language in such a way that it can be applied honestly and effectively in our present-day context. Thus it is reduced to the level of a foreign language which is sometimes used, but only in exceptional situations. As far as daily life is concerned, faith becomes largely speechless and consequently atrophied. For together with traditional Christian language, traditional forms of utterance such as sermons and prayer take on a special status which no longer permits an unconstrained use of them. And in this way uncertainty about language leads in the end to boredom with the Christian word. People become tired of using a language with which they have a troubled relationship.

Of course we shall not readily acquiesce in this perplexity. The fact that the impression has arisen that faith demands an intellectual achievement arouses the suspicion that the relationship between faith and language has been thought of in a way which overlooks the differences, is too much along traditional theoretical lines and is inadequately orientated towards experience. But there is no doubt that the problem as it is in fact largely posed today can be summed up by saying that, as a result of a troubled relationship to the traditional Christian language, boredom with words must spread rapidly. There is reason to suspect that we are touching here on the roots of a general situation at the present time. But we shall limit ourselves in the first instance to describing the symptoms of the crisis as they are manifested within Christianity. Here, in conclusion, is a brief account of this complex of familiar and often lamented experiences.

In the use of Christian language, whether in listening to it or in using it oneself, uncertainty and inhibitions are widespread. No one is seized by the word or filled by it. Only rarely and with difficulty is a genuine word achieved, a word with which the person who speaks it is in total agreement and which convinces and helps the person to whom it is spoken. That the word is food which gives and maintains life, a necessary sustenance for life, a word of life, is something that people are mostly aware of only historically, as a biblical statement. It is not confirmed and verified by their own experience. Accordingly the use of Christian language is disappearing. In general, the liturgical sermon remains in being because it is an institution. And there are still people who listen to sermons. And it would be a caricature if the sermon was described as something containing only repetition and soothing self-assurance. Of course there are people who are stuck in their rut, who merely recite correct dogmatic statements or familiar biblical sayings, and sometimes display an intolerable casualness in preparation and in the exercise of the responsibility of preaching. And likewise we can also find those whose attitude is that they only want to hear the usual thing and do not wish to be disturbed. Critical vigilance is then restricted to checking that all the right words are in the right place, and that the pious obligation of saying what is supposed to be said has been carried out.

But the matter should not be brushed aside with such clichés. In general, honest effort is put into the preparation of sermons. That Sunday morning worship is preceded by such an expenditure of intellectual effort, by self-torment at a task that is permanently too much, and sometimes by persistent struggles through the night to the limits of exhaustion with an incomplete manuscript, could well be regarded as an argument that all is clearly not well. Sometimes, again, an understandable disappointment often leads the hearer to avoid sharing the burden of such effort. People make general condemnations and overlook, amongst the mass of words, what might still attract the attention and provoke thought. Instead of at least *suffering* in the situation of the Christian proclamation of the word, people cut themselves off from the opportunity of such painful experiences.

Again, the statement that Christian language has been excluded from the public sphere and forced into the private realm is a half-truth. Certainly the world of work in its widest sense – that is, including politics, which has become a highly technical craft – is as it were sterilized against anything said about God. People have become extremely sensitive to any attempt to add Christian or any other kind of religious trimmings to the secular, and in certain respects this is right. On the other hand it is not the case that the language of faith is given a correspondingly satisfying welcome in the so-called private sector. On the contrary, the impression is that the place where Christian language is most easily able to maintain itself in being is in institutions publicly provided for the purpose such as church services, weddings and funerals, where one can use this language under the protection of the fact that it is expected. But in open personal discussion it is much more difficult to use explicitly Christian terms. And we can see in prayer above all how weak or even completely absent is the ability to make personal use of this language. People have come to accept that Christian language is in use only as something spoken by the competent specialist, and which he helplessly or fearfully offers them, but not as a language which is used with a spontaneous, constantly creative life of its own.

Here again, one must not descend to cheap caricature. To have something essential and helpful spelt out to one and to cling to it imitatively and even literally can in some circumstances be a salvation in extremity. But this too is a symptom of a troubled language situation: everything which is put forward by way of fixed language and established order (such as liturgical formulae, or the christenings, weddings and funerals which occur from time to time in the ordinary life of society) is regarded almost exclusively at the present day as likely to be emptied of meaning from long traditional use, and is therefore discredited, as something which takes away freedom. Such forms of language are treated as mere psychological and sociological mechanisms of compulsion. It is even regarded as suspicious merely to consider the possibility that they might have a meaningful use.

2. PRACTICAL ACTION

Boredom with words seems to find a justification and compensation, obvious in human terms and yet Christian too, in the shift of emphasis away from words towards action. While devout talk is judged by its fruits, and accordingly what is thought to matter are its effects in practical action, it does seem, looking at the history of Christianity as a whole, that the balance comes down against words. And this is so from both points of view, that of the hopeless impotence and that of the ominous power of words. As far as the impotence of words is concerned, an immense outpouring of words seems only to have served to interpret the world differently, instead of changing it. As far as the power of words is concerned, by means of words, existing social circumstances have been given sanction, real needs have been disguised by substitutes and necessary changes have actually been hindered. There is no doubt that this pattern of interpretation, which derives from the nineteenth-century criticism of religion and exercises such fascination at the present day, often brings suppressed facts to the surface and explains important issues. But it is also possible to make an ideological misuse of it – not in the first instance in the form of Marxism, but in the different liberal, puritan or clerical variants which make so much of practical action that the relevance of words is overlooked and there is a flight from responsibility for words to practical action.

As in the case of all polemical exaggerations, it is easy for people to overlook the fact that they are setting against each other things which are inseparable from each other and are interwoven with each other. It is perfectly obvious that human action, as a purposeful and meaningful activity, is dependent upon language. Action requires a previous judgment and is subject to a later judgment. Depending upon the circumstances, action must be taught, ordered, inculcated and impressed upon the memory. And in so far as words are aimed at action and have that purpose, they must of course go on to action. They become empty if they are not fulfilled by action. The same is of course true of discourse which actually purports to be about practical action: it is not necessarily proof against not resulting in practical action at all. But it is obvious that not every word must be judged by deeds. The scope of what is uttered in words is far wider than the sphere of action, unless the point is made that every utterance in words is itself an activity. In any case, no human action can exist without the element which gives life to everything human, language. Not that every action must be accompanied by words. There are situations in which the intervention of words cannot but be harmful, interfering with the action required; situations in which the act speaks for itself. On the other hand there are situations in which words purely as such (that is, simply by being spoken) represent an action and might well be distorted by further action. But the first case, in which acts become words, does not permit us to place a low value on what happens in language. For acts can become words only by virtue of language. In language reality is already in a sense contained, and the sphere of human life illuminated. Actions can only speak comprehensively because a sounding board of meaning is there to receive them, which gives words to the soundless act and makes it comprehensible.

We must in any case consider what 'practical action' really means. We must not limit it to work in the sense of an activity which produces something empirically tangible, of 'material re-actions between [man] and nature'.[2] This does not do justice to what practical action is, by contrast to a theoretical opinion, which keeps its actual situation in the background. That is, it is the reality of life itself. Of course from some points of view thought can simply be contrasted with action. Man is not then seen as a whole in either of these two human modes of behaviour. But it is possible to adopt a different starting point and make the distinction between a theoretical opinion, as an examination of the process of life from outside, and practical action in the form of life as it is actually lived. But in this case the theoretical attitude can be considered as a particular mode of human behaviour and to this extent as a particular concrete form (or from a different point of view again, as a particular abstraction) of the practical action of which human existence itself is constituted.

This is made clear in the ancient scholastic enquiry, whether

theology was a *scientia speculativa* or a *scientia practica*. Thomas
Aquinas says that it is both, though in such a way that the
primacy is given to the speculative element.[3] He was bound
to give this answer, because he took the concept of the practical
in the narrow sense of moral action. Consequently, to describe
it as a *scientia practica* would have made theology subject to
morality. But by emphasizing the speculative element, Thomas
gave the upper hand in matters of theology to the function of
receiving knowledge, which belongs to faith. As is well known,
Luther's answer to this traditional question was that theology
as such was *theologia practica*. This flatly excluded the understanding of it as *theologia speculativa*.[4] He in his turn was bound
to adopt this view, because for him the 'practical' signified
life as it has to be lived. But this meant that for him faith itself
was actually to be found on the side of practice, not because of
the works which follow it, but because in a fundamental way
faith itself is of decisive importance for life. For as Luther
describes it in the sermon 'On Good Works', faith is the
fulfilment of the first commandment, and therefore the source
of all good works – and this in so radical a sense that it is faith
alone which makes works good, because only faith can give a
good conscience and provide assurance.

This displays a view of man's human existence, according to
which the question about what man is cannot be answered by
reference to his actions. Rather, the actions raise the question
about what man is in a more acute form, that of the question
about the person who perpetrates them, the doer himself. But
the person who does the act is not constituted by his acts, but
by what calls him to do them, makes him capable of doing
them and determines that he shall act; and also by the judgment
to which he knows he is exposing himself by so doing. If one
follows Luther's own usage and calls this a passive element in
human existence, preceding and underlying the active, one
should not be disturbed by the pejorative associations of passiv-

ity. Luther does not mean a passivity which overcomes human existence or even eliminates personal existence altogether, but the passivity to which human existence owes its being and which constitutes personal existence. It is the kind of passivity that is contained in the statement 'I am loved'. It could be called an inspiring, life-giving passivity, the experience of which is in the highest sense an *actus* of man, and so determines his life and his practical action, for the very reason that it is not his *opus*.

Only if one ignores these ontological relationships does one fall prey to the foolish view that practical action and words must be opposed, and come to exaggerate the point of view of practical action through boredom with words. Properly understood, to take practical action seriously demands that words should be taken seriously. And genuine concentration on words necessarily brings with it a concentration on practice. Of course we must not treat lightly the caution implied in the expression 'properly understood'. That is, we must be clear what are the sources of the misunderstandings which obscure the issues and do so much damage. And we must realize that it can often seem right either to become the advocate of practical action against words (or more properly, against a distorted understanding of words and a use of words which ignores reality), or to become the advocate of words against practical action (or rather, against a restricted conception of practical action and against a practice which consequently does violence to life). And in order to clear the way for an account of theological language, a number of preliminary clarifications are necessary.

In the field of tension which is set up at the present day by the tendency for theological enthusiasm to be devoted not to words but to practical action, decisions of fundamental theology have to be made. There is absolutely no question that the confrontation of Christianity with the present circumstances of the world is irrevocable. One might even say that it is necessary of its very nature. For Christian faith itself implies a universal mission to the world. It would be contradictory to its nature if one were to affirm Christian faith, but ignore the world, to take no account of its circumstances and ills, to cut oneself off from the disturbing, provoking, alarming claim made by the undisguised and undiluted apprehension of the world. If faith is really faith in Jesus, it places the believer where Jesus is and seeks to be: amongst the sick, the hungry and thirsty, the outcasts of society, those who need love, but who according to human judgment are not worthy of love. And this definition of the place where Christianity is to be found is not removed by the exaltation of Jesus Christ to the right hand of God, but on the contrary is confirmed and irrevocably brought into force as the essence of God's love for the world. But if this is so, then Christian faith will allow nothing to surpass it in its burning passion to share in the suffering of the world. In spite of this, there are Christians who sleep or wilfully close their eyes, because it looks as though faith can only be maintained if it is protected against the disturbing aspects of what takes place in the world by a retreat into an introverted inner life. Where this is so, the other voices, which give utterance to the suppressed facts, are unquestionably in the right – even where they speak the language of recklessness, party strife and hatred, the primordial sounds, as it were, of the outcry of a suffering creation. This does not mean that we should join in such utterances of recklessness, party strife and hatred in the name of faith. What really matters is whether faith has anything to utter other than the mere cry of the suffering creation, and whether it has anything more to say than to proclaim and advocate measures for changing the situation of the world which could best be put forward in the name of reason.

Of course a judicious balance in the observation and judgment of the situation of the world brings with it the risks, or at least the suspicion, that one is doing nothing more than deceitfully knocking off the corners and sharp edges of a hard and confused reality, neutralizing tensions, crippling the will to intervene decisively and thereby blocking the way to practical action. This must be admitted. Anyone who wants to get anything done cannot go on for ever wondering where to start. Without delay he must apply himself to what comes his way, and if necessary take the risk of making a mistake. He must not hesitate to get his hands dirty, and perhaps even to incur guilt. If necessary, he even has to act when he cannot see the consequences, and must accept the fear of having evil consequences on his conscience in any given case. But it is one thing to know this and even to reveal that one knows it, and another thing fanatically to exclude the very thought of it and in the interests of effectiveness and power to advocate a criticism which tolerates no criticism itself.

To attack this tangled problem with a very simple basic statement, Christian faith is a liberation from fanaticism. The fact that in the history of Christianity fanaticism has produced strange and even terrible effects only emphasizes how much Christian faith is a subject of dispute even in history, and how much it is in conflict with a caricature of itself. Of course it is easier and at first sight more effective to have Christianity fly a party banner in the present situation of the world, to enrol it on the side of anti-communism or anti-Americanism or Maoism, instead of taking on the task of fighting fanaticism between the opposing lines of battle. It is a short-sighted view that only fanaticism can be effectively committed to a cause, and that the burning problems of the world at the present day are taken seriously only if one accepts the patterns, slogans and historical constructions which already exist. The service which a Christian is called upon to carry out in the first instance, and which should not be undertaken lightly, is to recognize concrete needs with the vigilant eye of love, and therefore without fanaticism, and, in the knowledge of the limits which are imposed on knowledge and even more on action, to commit himself fully to the immediate tasks.

The way the relationship of theology to practical action is understood decides whether the call for practical action gives point to the theme of theology or whether it loses sight of it and replaces it by a different theme. There must be clear criteria in order to judge in any given case whether theology is still at work on its proper task. Of course a formal appeal to the proper subject of theology is not enough, and the specific matter of which this consists must be more precisely defined.

3. THE SUBJECT MATTER OF THEOLOGY

The fact that people so often and so readily use the formal expression 'the subject of theology' has a more profound reason than the fact that it is easy simply to offer an empty framework which can be changed for another, instead of tying oneself down to a clearly defined picture. For the subject matter of theology can be expressed in more than one way. However it is formulated or described by implication, there are a thousand and one possibilities of putting it differently. The range of differences extends from statements which are actually con-tradictory, through all kinds of qualifications and changes of emphasis, to expressions which are synonymous. This draws our attention to an extraordinarily important aspect of the problem of language from the theological point of view. The reason for this multiplicity is not the simple one, that every-thing which can be said in matters of theology is after all beyond logical demonstration, impossible to check, unverifiable and, if subjected to a rigorous standard of language, perhaps even meaningless. However important the problems implied by this suggestion, the first cause of this multiplicity which we must consider is that it is only possible to state what the subject of theology is in language which changes with the course of history; and therefore the statement must constantly be made anew. And even though traditional language may have a creative and normative function in this, this in its turn comes to us in a polyphony of astonishing complication, and not as the unaccompanied melody of a language which is a unity.

Now we must point out that the language of ordinary discourse is always faced with this problem. It is subject to history, and indeed itself – in a sense which we shall not go into at the moment – is the cause of historical change. This is the cause of the variability and imprecision of language, its ambiguity, and also of the possibility of multiple synonymity. It is often possible to express the same thing differently without affecting the identity of meaning. And it is often necessary to do this, in order to preserve identity of meaning where the conditions of understanding vary. All this is not exclusively true of theology, but it is true of theology as well. It is subject to the general fate of language. But what makes the problem more acute in the case of theology, and threatens to turn the complexity of language into a hopeless confusion of language, is the difficulty already mentioned, which must never be underestimated, of reaching agreement about theological statements, of testing them against the phenomenon itself, of verifying them or proving them false.

But the mere combination of these two points of view, the historical variability of language and what we may call for the moment the religious and metaphysical intangibility of theological statements, is not sufficient to sum up the character-istic content of the problem of theological language. We first come to the heart of the problem when we consider the relation between what history is concerned with and what faith is concerned with. One might suppose that the subject of theology is not affected by two completely different and indeed conflict-

ing causes of language problems, but that a single issue of
content determined the problem of language we have to
consider. Certain things would follow if this were the case. It
would not be possible, as the current view supposes, to play
off the allegedly conflicting historical outlook and the point
of view of faith. Nor would it be possible to imagine that the
conflict could be resolved by means of the familiar schematic
distinction which represents the historical as a horizontal
dimension and the genuinely theological as a vertical dimension.
According to this schematic pattern, statements about God are
only to be drawn into the movement of history as the result of a
mistake or fault, and are really incommensurate with it by the
very fact that they are *statements* about God. But according to
the Christian understanding statements about God stand or
fall by their relevance to the world as history, by being themselves historical and, being history, by being therefore relevant
to the world. And here all the threads of the problem of
theological language are joined together. Consequently we
can expect that the multiplicity of language which gives us
such trouble in our attempt to determine the proper subject of
theology should not be regarded as a disadvantage and as an
unfortunate consequence of the historical nature of language.
It is clearly involved in a process of cause and effect with the
historical life and exercise of faith, and belongs itself to the
proper subject of theology. Consequently – and here we return
from our brush with the deeper levels of the problem of
theological language to the main line of our argument – it is
easy to understand the tendency to withhold comment on the
process of language involved by means of the formal expression
'the subject of theology'. It shows a desire, quite appropriate
to the subject of theology, not violently to restrict or even to
bring to a standstill, by means of a rigid formula, the movement
which is appropriate to the subject matter of theology, but
instead to keep consideration of it in motion and to give it

elbow-room. For it is concerned with something which cannot be brought to conclusion by means of a formula.

But it is of course necessary to make clear statements about the content of the subject matter of theology. Only then can one go on to decide what is the right understanding of the relation of theology to practical action. Looking back to our digression above, it seems best not to answer the question of the subject matter of theology by means of a clearly defined formula. One could do so, and no doubt express something of the truth. But it would not immediately be applicable as a criterion, because good reasons would exist to propose other formulas. Even the classical answers to the question of the subject matter of theology (or as it used to be called, with a different terminological nuance, the *subiectum* of theology) were not basically intended to lay down certain dogmatic principles, which were to be regarded as the most important, but were rather intended to delineate the situation in which the matter of theology was as it were 'in play'. That is, they were intended to determine the situation in life to which all theological statements are to be related. Thus the statement of content which was sought from them becomes a statement of place. But it would be a misunderstanding to suppose that this again leaves us still in the purely formal sphere. The statement of place defines the stage on which the matter of theology is acted out; or to express it differently, determines the combination of elements which make up the event to which theology relates as its subject matter.

The scholastic answer to the question of the *subiectum theologiae* was that God was the *subiectum* of theology.[5] It did not intend to state *materialiter* the sole object which theology discusses, nor was it even proposing *a parte potiori* its principal object, above but in addition to others. God here is rather, to use the technical term, being called the *ratio formalis*, that is the point of view from which alone everything else is considered which may occur in theology. And this can include virtually anything within the whole range from the creation to the end of the world, from life to death, from heaven to hell! The concentration on God includes a multitude of other relationships: to be destined by God, to owe existence to him, to be subject to his judgment, to be accepted by him, to be exalted by him, to be united with him. This multiple process, in which the relationship to God takes place between God as the beginning and God as the end of all things, is the subject of theology. And what is not considered from the point of view of this *ratio formalis* is not being discussed theologically.

That the subject matter of theology concerns something that happens is made even more clear by Luther's polarizing definition of the object of theology as 'guilty and lost man and the justifying and redeeming God'.[6] It would be a superficial interpretation of this understanding if it were taken merely to refer to a single doctrine, the doctrine of justification, as if in determining the content of theology priority were being given to what seems to be only part of its dogmatic content. One might suspect that an arbitrary choice was being made, the symptom of a sectarian mode of thought. What objection can there be, from this point of view, when others make the main issue questionable marginal matters such as the thousand-year kingdom, the keeping of the sabbath or a rigorist ethic? Or when, to avoid giving the impression of caricature, such unquestionably central themes as the commandment to love one's neighbour, the doctrine of the vicarious suffering of Christ or the conception of the kingdom of God are regarded as of greater importance for the subject matter of theology than the doctrine of justification? Even if one can agree with this brief formula, *homo reus et perditus et Deus iustificans vel salvator*, with some demurral, as a useful indicator, it seems to lack a good deal. It does not even mention Jesus Christ. It says nothing about new life. It sounds individualistic, and seems wholly to exclude our relationship with our fellow men, and so forth. But such considerations do not do justice to the formula. Its purpose is not to give preference to a particular doctrinal statement, but to outline the basic structure of the content of theology itself. It presents as the specific subject of theology the situation of man in the sight of God. And it does so directly from the point of view of the event which is determined and fulfilled by this situation: the restoration of a disturbed and indeed destroyed relationship; that is, the event of atonement, of reconciliation, of the return from damnation to salvation, from the destruction of life to the affirmation of life. It is not a fortuitous situation but the basic situation of man, enveloping and penetrating his whole life, which serves here as an indication of when and how the subject matter of theology touches upon life, and how it becomes 'practical' in a fundamental sense. What the statement means is therefore that everything which is not discussed from this point of view and in the context of this event is not being discussed *theologically*. And this is true even when statements are made about God, but not about God with regard to *this* event, this turning from what seems to be an ultimate negation to an unrepeatable and definitive affirmation. Thus this statement of locality provides a criterion for identifying what is truly theological in all possible theological statements. Other theological statements as such have to demonstrate what their situation in life is with the aid of this statement.

A third example of a definition of the subject matter of theology can be found in a remark by Schleiermacher. I must go into greater detail here, because what is at issue is not immediately obvious. But this very example reveals perspectives which are extremely illuminating for the question of the relationship of theology to practical action, and the connection between that relationship and the phenomenon of boredom with words. In considering the structure of the doctrine of faith in his second *Synodic Letter to Lücke* Schleiermacher remarks: 'I would have liked to arrange that as far as possible it would be clear to the readers at every point that the saying in John 1: 14 is the basic text of the whole of dogmatic theology, just as it must also be for the whole ministry of a clergyman.'[7] The point of this statement is aimed against the misunderstanding that the doctrine of faith rests upon a speculative basis. He proposes instead John 1: 14 ('The Word became flesh and dwelt among us, full of grace and truth; we have beheld his glory, glory as of the only Son from the Father') as the basic text of the whole of dogmatic theology. One might regard this, in view of the desire to avoid any suspicion of a tendency to speculation, as the expression of a determined attempt to direct theology towards practical action. But Schleiermacher does not mean it in this sense. In fact in the context we have quoted he uses the expression rather to reject it. He does not wish for the subject with which he is concerned to be confused with what are known as 'practical dogmatics'. This is something for which Schleiermacher has little regard, and which is sometimes tacked on to true dogmatic theology when the latter is felt to be too theoretical, so that it should not seem too cold and dry. Schleiermacher looks for as little from such a relationship to practical action, tacked on as an afterthought, as from the attempt to proceed straight from the scholarly treatment of dogmatic theology in a lecture to an edifying discourse, which would in fact endanger its scholarly content.

This rejection of practical theology as something tacked on afterwards is not directed against the relationship of theology to practical action but rather against trying to establish it in so unsatisfactory a way. When Schleiermacher made his well-known statement that practical theology is the crown of theology, he meant that it is that towards which all the forces and sap in the tree are flowing;[8] and this is the movement which should determine the whole structure of dogmatic theology, and should be at work in the tone of all its statements.

It does not seem at first sight convincing that John 1: 14 should be used to express this, as the basic text of dogmatic theology. For here we are obviously being referred to a particular theological statement, that of the incarnation of the *logos*, something which seems to be in formal contradiction to the conception of practical action as well as to the usual conception of Schleiermacher's theological thought. What Schleiermacher means by this reference can be explained by isolating three aspects which are closely related to it.

Firstly, he wishes to emphasize that Christianity is a faith in which everything is related 'to the redemption accomplished by Jesus of Nazareth'.[9] Thus, in the face of the suspicion that dogmatic theology is based speculatively on a natural theology, a pantheist conception of God or the like, he wishes to make clear that its essential element is a relationship to a quite specific historical event, the appearance of Jesus of Nazareth. He would have preferred to reverse the way in which his dogmatic theology was in fact structured and build it up from this Christocentric starting point; but this would have brought with it other disadvantages which, because of the current temptations that assailed the Church, would have had a harmful effect upon church life, and therefore upon practical action.[10]

For – and this is the second aspect – Christianity is a faith which is wholly and completely orientated towards life. And its understanding of life is such that in it the natural in human conditions is subordinate to the moral.[11] In terms of the phenomenology of religion, Schleiermacher expresses this in the phrase 'teleological religion'. By this he means that 'a predominating reference to the moral task constitutes the fundamental type of the religious affections'.[12] He thereby rejects a purely aesthetic understanding of Christianity. 'In the realm of Christianity the consciousness of God is always related to the totality of active states in the idea of a Kingdom of God. As for the idea of a beauty of the soul, regarded as the result of all the influences of Nature and the world, this has always remained so foreign to Christianity (in spite of Christianity's early absorption of Hellenism *en masse*) that it has never been adapted into the cycle of current expressions in the realm of Christian piety, and has never been maintained in any treatise of Christian morals. But that figure of a Kingdom of God, which is so important and indeed all-inclusive for Christianity, is simply the general expression of the fact that in Christianity all pain and all joy are religious only in so far as they are related to activity in the Kingdom of God, and that every religious emotion which proceeds from a passive state ends in the consciousness of a transition to activity.'[13] It would be a complete misunderstanding of Schleiermacher's intention to interpret this as ethical in Kant's sense, as the reduction of religion to morality. The conception of morality is wider here, and he understands the subordination of the natural to the moral in a different way from Kant. But, above all, the autonomy of the religious self-consciousness is not understood as its separation from the other expressions of life, but as that which determines the whole of human existence, and in this sense is inclined in the direction of morality. Here there is an understanding of practical action which includes the whole scope of the process of life and does not limit it to a handful of specific forms of activism. Only in this way can Schleiermacher make John 1: 14 the watchword of an understanding of theology directed towards practical action. For, as opposed to an intellectualist understanding of the *logos*, the incarnation of the *logos* means that life itself has become the place of the presence and the experience of his glory, a *doxa*, the riches of which are grace and truth. For Schleiermacher this event of incarnation is the basis of the relation of theology to practical action.

And there is also a third aspect, which concerns the relationship between the word and practice. And in so far as the word is simply taken to mean a fixed statement, while practice means life itself, Schleiermacher firmly emphasizes 'that the statements are only derivative and the inward state of mind the original'.[14] In this remark, which directly precedes his reference to John 1: 14 as the basic text of the whole of dogmatic theology, Schleiermacher is not proposing that a low value should be placed on words. Such an attitude would in any case scarcely be reconcilable with the power of thought, and the care and precision of language, which Schleiermacher applied in an almost ascetic way to dogmatic theology. Nor is he talking about an inner life which ignores the connection with practical action. On the contrary, his reference to the inward state of mind as the original is meant to ensure a proper understanding of practical action and a right relationship to it. And finally, Schleiermacher has no intention of making the religious self-consciousness an autonomous source of theological statements. In immediate juxtaposition to the reference John 1: 14 this would be grotesque. But the conception that Jesus of Nazareth is the ultimate source and point of reference of all theological statements is only protected against speculative or dogmatic misuse if the life that proceeds from him makes it possible to trace theological statements back to utterances of faith and to judge them by it. It also makes it possible not to accept the utterances of faith externally as alien elements, which subsequently have to be appropriated inwardly in some way or another, but instead to understand them and adopt them as one's own on the basis of the life from which they derive. And therefore it is very important for Schleiermacher that John 1: 14 is not only the basic text of dogmatic theology but at the same time of the whole ministry of the clergyman. That is, it gives guidance for the whole practice of the Church, though that is still a matter of dealing responsibly with the word.

Let us now look back and relate what we have learnt about

Schleiermacher to what we saw in the other examples of the formulation of the subject matter of theology, those of Thomas Aquinas and Luther. We realize that such a formulation cannot be a matter simply of setting up a dogmatic statement on its own as a summary of the content of theology. This is certainly not Schleiermacher's intention when he calls John 1: 14 the basic text of the whole of dogmatic theology. Nor does he want to prescribe a kind of minimal confession of faith, which can be trotted out as a shibboleth of orthodoxy whenever a mistrustful fellow Christian asks for the password. What he intends is to show the inner structure of the subject matter of theology: the life with which it is concerned, the place where and the way in which its heart beats. In other words, he is trying to make clear what takes place when one really gets to work on the subject matter of theology, and sizes it up without being distracted, instead of losing sight, in the midst of a forest of individual theological subjects, of the one thing with which theology is really concerned.

4. CRITERIA

It is not, however, enough to rest content with classical answers to the question of the subject matter of theology, however much the interpretation of them leads one to reconsider them, give a degree of consent and take them further. Not for the sake of originality at any price, but in order to give as honest and precise a personal account as possible, we will now set out a number of criteria which can be used to see whether theology is dealing with its proper subject matter. What our historical examples reveal will be of value to us in this. We shall limit ourselves to a number of focal points which illuminate our main problems: the phenomenon of boredom with language and the controversial relationship of theology to practical action. Because I limit myself to the question of the conditions under which theology is out of touch with its theme, the form of the criteria which I propose will be only negative. But the way will be left open for the consideration of a positive definition of the proper subject of theology. I group my remarks under three headings: the presence of the hidden, the situation in which words are spoken, and the changing of the world.

a. The Presence of the Hidden

Theology loses touch with its theme when statements about God no longer seem indispensable to it. This is a tautology as long as one sticks to the literal definition of theology. To understand theology as what its name requires is of course something which nowadays can no longer be taken for granted. There are people who believe it possible to put forward a theology without God. But the effect of this is more to conceal difficulties by dialectic and to increase confusion than to advance understanding and help to solve the problem of language. But if we continue to hold the view that the subject matter of theology would be abandoned if statements about God were no longer to appear indispensable, then we must give a reason why statements about God are necessary. The phrase 'the presence of the hidden' is meant to point towards this. We might also have used the concept of mystery.[15]

'The presence of the hidden' indicates what the decisive function and power of language consists of. It makes present what would not be immediately obvious. The function of language, therefore, is seen in a particularly impressive way in its power of transcending the present moment. It is able to make present what no longer exists and what does not yet exist. Without language we would have no relationship with the past and the future; we would be imprisoned in the present moment and banished to our very immediate environment. The same is true of the transcendence that leads to the whole complex of circumstances in which what is immediately present to us is located, and from there to what it signifies, what is proclaimed in it and the thoughts it provokes.

The word 'God' brings to utterance the mystery of reality as such. To this extent it represents the most extreme and, if I might so put it, the most pure possibility of language. In it language affirms the presence of what is completely hidden, and therefore does what only words can do. Consequently the problem of language and the question of God are very closely interwoven. Statements about God pose to an extreme degree the question of one's responsibility for the language which one uses. And to look at the question the other way round: the consideration of language itself leads to the problem of how the unutterable can be uttered. To give up the word 'God' would mean to give up being concerned with the mystery of reality. But this means that the word 'God' is only rightly used if it does not draw man away from the experience of reality, but makes him open to it, relating him to the whole continuum of reality. The word 'God' would be used contrary to what it implies, if it denoted an isolated object, instead of referring to reality as a whole. To speak about God means to speak about reality as a whole and therefore to speak about man, who is exposed to reality as a whole. Here again the reverse is true: to speak about God is to deny that one can speak about the world as a whole as such, by speaking *only* about the world, or that one can speak about man as such at all by speaking about nothing other than man. If theology does not come to terms with the scope of this whole continuum, it has abandoned its theme. This does not mean that the problems we have mentioned – whether they are expounded in the language of religion or of metaphysics or of a philosophy of language – themselves actually form the theme of theology in a strict sense. Indeed, when theology brings to utterance its specific theme, it must exercise a highly critical vigilance with regard to such general reflections. But it can speak on its own proper subject only if it comes to grips with the refractory matter in the experience of reality, and we might also say in the experience of language, represented by the word 'God'.

b. The Situation in which Words are Spoken

Theology loses touch with its theme when it abandons the category of the individual. If, in reaction against a real or supposed individualism, expressions such as inner life, conscience and the like are placed on an 'index of forbidden words', with the intention of excluding altogether the aspects of the problem they refer to, this is a failure to recognize the nature of the situation in which words are spoken. The concept of the situation in which words are spoken is an indication, with regard to what happens when words are uttered, that we must guard against looking at things in isolation. For the effect of this on theology is bound to be destructive; and not on theology alone.

Where words are uttered, the most wide-ranging links with our fellow men and with existence as it is in the world are necessarily associated with the utterance. We could not speak and understand language if language had not been uttered to us in advance, drawing us into the continuum of language which existed before us and independently of us. Man owes his existence – quite apart from the question of God – not to himself, but to a community of men. The manifestations and effects of this community of course include, to some extent as the primary element, what is nowadays known, somewhat one-sidedly and misleadingly, as society. Similarly, utterance in language would not be possible at all without the expectation of being heard and understood, without the possibility of participating and exchanging in the shared subjectivity and interdependence of social reality. Consequently language would be empty, and would lack any content of utterance, if a reality already experienced was not always preserved in it and spoken through it, and a new experience of reality revealed – that is, if language did not mediate the world. To take seriously the point of view of the situation in which words are spoken means something else as well. It means to be conscious that every statement has its context from which it can be distinguished, but with which it forms a living unity. Consequently a statement can often say much more than it makes explicit. It can be understood better than would be the case if it were taken at face value. And it can lose credibility if it contradicts the behaviour of the person who speaks it.

The concept of the situation in which words are spoken reminds us of all these phenomena, because they are of decisive importance for the understanding of what happens when words are uttered. But they would lose their substance, the centre of their life, if it were not realized that every statement must pass through the needle's eye of the individual if it is to take the form of real words. Think how words ever come to be spoken and answered. Consider how hearing and understanding actually take place. Consider what the word ultimately achieves, what it is capable of bringing about, giving and denying, and what one can fail to do and lack with regard to words. In every case one comes up against the relationship in which the individual as such comes to have significance by virtue of the inextricable links which bind him to his fellow men and the world as a whole. And one sees that the relationship to society, and the relationship to the world, which are the specific human relationships, are maintained only when the individual is taken seriously. Theology has a special obligation to accept responsibility for this being done. For in his existence in the sight of God man is an individual in the extreme sense, and it is precisely this which makes the most powerful claim upon his relationship to his fellow men and his responsibility for the world, and calls him to exercise them.

c. The Changing of the World

Theology loses touch with its theme if it is not concerned with that which completely changes the world. Amongst the objections to theology are those which call for a radical changing of the world. In answer to these objections, theology must demonstrate that it is indeed theology not by calling for a change in a watered-down form, or pushing it out of sight, but by advocating it in its most radical form. But there immediately arises the question of what standard is to be applied. And this question divides into two related questions. What does it mean to change the world in every respect? And what part has the business of theology to play in bringing about such a change?

To begin with the latter, it is clear that the work of theology is not directly to change the world. It bears comparison with other academic activities (including literature and art). Of course we know that research in the natural sciences can result in astounding changes in the world, but only when it is associated with technology and the whole complex of economic and political interests. Philosophical thought can have epoch-making effects. But it does not itself directly undertake action to change the world. In fact one may ask whether philosophical thought does not merely follow a change which has taken place at an even deeper level, and simply gives expression to it.

According to Hegel: 'Philosophy . . . is its own time apprehended in thoughts',[16] and he elaborated this in a way which seems extremely sceptical with regard to the question of the changing of the world. 'One more word about giving instruction as to what the world ought to be. Philosophy in any case always comes on the scene too late to give it. As the thought of the world, it appears only when actuality is already there cut and dried after its process of formulation has been completed. The teaching of the concept, which is also history's inescapable lesson, is that it is only when actuality is mature that the ideal first appears over against the real and that the ideal apprehends this same real world in its substance and builds it up for itself into the shape of an intellectual realm. When philosophy paints its grey in grey, then has a shape of life grown old. By philosophy's grey in grey, it cannot be rejuvenated but only understood. The owl of Minerva spreads its wings only with the falling of the dusk.'[17] But when Karl Marx, in his famous eleventh thesis against Feuerbach, says: 'The philosophers have only interpreted the world in different ways; the point is to *change* it',[18] this statement, in so far as it is directed in particular against Hegel, misrepresents Hegel's opinion. For Hegel argued that the self-awareness of the spirit goes on to produce a further development, so that philosophy can be called 'the birthplace of the spirit' which was 'later to appear in its true form'. And Hegel adduces as a profound example of this 'that what Greek philosophy was, appeared in reality in the Christian world'.[19] But quite apart from the way in which Hegel understood the relationship between philosophy and history, one cannot accept a simple antithesis between 'interpreting the world' and 'changing the world', however attractive it may sound. In so far as changes in the interpretation of the world consist of really important insights, they are not a matter of chance whims and notions, but are caused by the hidden movement at a profound level which largely underlies historical changes. But no one involved in these changes can anticipate and plan the course they will take or what they will bring about. Moreover, the process of interpretation as the achievement of knowledge and understanding of the world always brings with it, potentially at least, a changing of the world. And false interpretations, of course, can have an extraordinary influence on history. Even the conservative refusal to recognize that changes in the world have taken place makes its own specific contribution to the changing of the world. And the revolutionary changing of the world, perhaps more than any other, derives from a new interpretation of the world, or at least makes use of it. The historical importance of Karl Marx himself rests exclusively upon the power of his words.

Now everything that can be said of scholarly and intellectual activity in general, with regard to the changing of the world, can also be applied to theology. Infrequently enough, and perhaps more rarely than elsewhere in history, the history of theology also contains turning points, at which changes of epoch-making importance take place, and these shape history for centuries after. It is unnecessary to give examples. But at the same time, of course, the history of theology, like all other history, is full of the small-scale and rapidly changing events which are much more a product of the changing of the world than a force which brings it about. But in spite of these similarities there is a distinctive feature which is associated with the understanding of the changing of the world appropriate to the subject matter of theology, and which accordingly defines the function of theology with regard to the changing of the world.

The concern of theology is with something which is in total contradiction to the view that nothing ever changes, and that consequently we ought to be content to leave things just as they are. For theology is concerned in an ultimate causal sense with what is new: with what is irrevocably new, never grows old, and makes new in a final sense. It brings the message of the new covenant and tells of the new man, new life, a new creation, a new heaven and a new earth. The theme of theology is a change in every respect. The expressions it uses describe the change from the old to the new in the most radical possible form, as the forgiveness of guilt, atonement, redemption, rebirth and resurrection. But the important thing here is this: the change in every respect is not something left to the future, so that everything is looked for in what is yet to come. Of course Christian faith implies hope, but this is a hope which is rooted in the faith that the world *has been* changed by Jesus Christ. This perfect tense, both indicative and causative with regard to what is absolutely new, has to be understood as a present perfect, as something which is still happening, and which lasts as long as this life and this world. The changing of the world to which it refers affects death in a twofold sense, not eliminating it and yet overcoming it. What is new is in fact consummated through and beyond death. This emphasizes how radical a changing of the world is intended here. It is not a changing of the world which is brought to its consummation under the limits of the conditions of the present world. Consequently, it leaves behind it all revolutionary upheavals in what exists here and now, for these are necessarily limited by the conditions of the present world.

Theology would have lost contact with its proper subject matter if it were not open to the suspicion of talking of a changing of the world in so radical a sense as to leave any practicable and attainable changing of the world out of the question. For it speaks in fact of a change which is not exhausted by the changing of historical circumstances. Nowadays, of course, the emphasis is placed in the other direction. Care is taken to protect the understanding of this change from an inwardness which alters nothing in the external situation. The change that is necessary, it is claimed, is not one of the heart alone, but also and above all of the situation. There are good and evident reasons for emphasizing that a change in circumstances is necessary. There is no question about this. But it is also clear that not every change in circumstances is a gain in itself. The increasing rate of such historical changes in a modern age, and especially the spectacular social, political and technical changes in the world during the twentieth century, can all be seen in the same light. In spite of all the upheavals everything is still basically the same. Though the circumstances have changed, often to an astonishing extent, the story of the old Adam continues. But even social changes which deal with obvious grievances and bring about a real improvement in people's lives are open to question when looked at critically. Apart from the price that often has to be paid for them, because of the damage they cause in other respects, they may well be open to the abuse which comes from the fact that even in the best of circumstances men can behave in an extremely evil way. But if the uncertainty factor of human behaviour is excluded as far as possible by circumstances which function reliably and perfectly, then in spite of the humane purpose which is at work here, the result is the very opposite to that desired and life is robbed of its humanity.

But here, without doubt, is the point of contact of the changing of the world which is inextricably bound up with the name of Jesus Christ. Theology would have lost contact with its proper subject matter if it abandoned the view that all that matters in the end is not the spectacular changes, but those which take place in concealment; not the changing of circumstances but the changing of man himself. And theology must apply this standard to any change in the circumstances, both to the coming about of that change, and to what results from it. The allergy which words like the heart, the conscience or the inner life produce in many theologians nowadays must be taken seriously as the symptom of a disease which may well be entirely due to a misuse of these words. But one should not confuse the avoidance of them, which perhaps is justified, with the therapy that is necessary.

In order to keep theology in touch with its proper subject matter, it is necessary to consider what basically takes place in the process for which the word 'gospel' is used. Here we have to avoid the danger of reinterpreting the gospel moralistically in two directions. The first mistake is the danger of changing its meaning to that of an ideal of virtue, which falsely expects from man as an achievement what he can have only as something imparted to him and received by him in thankful dependence – that is, freedom as the object of liberation and love as being loved. The second mistake is to change the meaning of the gospel to the activism of a social gospel, which at best is to confuse the fruits with the tree which produces them, and promotes acts of love without paying attention to the threat to the freedom to love. If theology understands the basic principle of what is required to change the world in accordance with the spirit of the gospel, it has no need to adopt an attitude of fearful timidity or ingratiating self-abasement, either towards psychology and educational theory or towards social morality and politics. One can then turn one's attention, impartially but with critical vigilance, to the fact that, and the way in which, the content of faith has something to do with general mental and social problems, needs and tasks, and yet is different from these. Theology can and indeed must take into account the processes with which psychology and the social sciences are concerned, each in their own way. It is not possible to speak of a changing of the world if the reality of the world is not taken into account. But theology must not make the standards applied in these subjects (in so far as one can speak of any such in this general way) the criteria of the subject matter of theology. That is, the relevance of the subject of theology must not be measured solely by, or reduced to, its relevance to social processes.

The function which is peculiar to theology itself is related to the theological understanding of the changing of the world. Theology is neither self-generating nor self-fulfilling. It ministers to a process of language that takes place outside itself. It is tied to and dependent upon a particular tradition, the essence of which is that the world *has been* changed by Jesus Christ. And it is always related to the proclamation and living out of this tradition; for there, what took place through Jesus Christ is still an event. Theology as such is not identical with this real life process. It could not even exist unless the events represented by the tradition were not already taking place both prior to and parallel with theology, bringing theology into being as one of the numerous expressions of its life.

An essential element in this tradition – that is, to sum it up in a formula, of Jesus Christ as an event which changes the world – is that it takes the form of words. This does not simply mean that something handed down from the past is made a present reality by being spoken. This is only true in a restricted sense. A tradition can also continue to have a living form in the attitudes and patterns of behaviour found in institutions and customs. There are of course examples of this in the way in which the Christian tradition has been maintained in being. This, however, is not the proper form of its tradition, nor can it be, because it is a tradition which is concerned with opening the way to the freedom to love – which means faith! But this setting free is a mental event which is always dependent upon words. This includes everything that was summed up as the 'the presence of the hidden', and also everything which we described under the heading of the 'situation in which words are spoken'. When we speak of tradition handed down in words, we are referring to the whole range of the way in which words come to be uttered. Thus it must not be reduced merely to a matter of speaking and repeating. We must also take into account the process in life in terms of which words that are received are seen to make sense, to which they apply, and in which they are therefore experienced. Perhaps the most adequate description of all that this means is to say that the receiving of words which takes place and produces its effects here should be understood as a reception in which life is handed on by witnesses to life. Thus the process of tradition with which theology is concerned must not be limited to what we are accustomed to associate with the conceptions, frequently most inadequate, of institutionalized tradition by the use of terms such as 'preaching' or the word 'Church'. Rather, it consists of the whole range of what Schleiermacher, in the great section of his 'Doctrine of Faith'[20] on pneumatology and ecclesiology, headed 'On the Constitution of the World with regard to the Redemption'. But because the maintenance and expression of the Christian tradition is so inextricably rooted in the world, primacy of place must be given to words, in order to preserve the most characteristic feature of what the tradition has to hand on, the bringing about of freedom to love.

For this same reason theology is necessary here to guard the purity of this process of tradition. To keep it pure means to keep in being the distinction, and therefore the real and effective link, between the radical changing of the world on the one hand, and relative changes in the world on the other. The nature of the radical changing of the world is that of the freedom which overcomes the world, freedom in the face of all the pressures which constrain us in the world. But the relative changing of the world, when it is justified, that is, when it is for the good of the world, derives from the freedom to love, and leaves room for it. It is a freedom which does not experience the commitment to service as a painful restriction, but in this very commitment fulfils itself as freedom. This distinction is parallel to that between what is God's affair and what is man's. It is God's affair to liberate man, so that he is simply and utterly dependent upon God, and thereby to place him in his right relationship to the world. But it is man's affair to exercise this responsibility for the world entrusted to him and to use it for the good of his fellow man and to the praise of God. It is the task of theology to guard this distinction and in this way to assist the expression and utterance of the tradition and to play an indirect part in this. It is not the task of theology to develop a theoretical programme to be put into practice as specific concrete actions. In fact the situation is best expressed by describing theology as a theory of language. For the practical action to which theology is related and which it serves itself takes place in the form of language. And because it is so extraordinarily wide-ranging, extending to the whole of life and every circumstance in the world, it is a language process which is more than any other subject to danger, and for this reason needs the self-critical discipline of a theory of language.

These observations on the third criterion of the subject matter of theology are very wide-ranging, and yet at the same time will be regarded as particularly inadequate. For here is the very heart of the problem, the reason which required us to go more deeply into the question of the subject of theology and set up some guide-lines. But a readiness to state what the proper subject of theology is, itself requires us to tackle this subject matter, and so to undertake an inexhaustible task. Even though we have had to limit ourselves here to pointing out where the problem lies and to laying down a few criteria, we have been unable to avoid touching on the sore points and consequently making extremely contentious statements. There is no harm in this, if it is true that anyone who wants to argue about the subject matter of theology must show his hand in regard to these points, because it is on these issues that he seeks assent.

Thus in advance of all detailed disagreement, we can at least agree that theology has lost contact with its proper theme if it is no longer concerned with what is implied in the phrases 'the presence of the hidden', 'the situation in which words are spoken' and 'the changing of the world'.

5. THE CRISIS OF LANGUAGE

Let us now return again to our starting point, the experience of boredom with words. One cannot but have a sympathetic understanding for the view – expressed in various tones of voice – that enough sermons have been preached, and that it would be much better to keep silence and to act. I need only to refer to the well-known statement by Dietrich Bonhoeffer: 'Our church, which has been fighting in these years only for its self-preservation, as though that were an end in itself, is incapable of taking the word of reconciliation and redemption to mankind and the world. Our earlier words are therefore bound to lose their force and cease, and our being Christians today will be limited to two things: prayer and righteous action among men. All Christian thinking, speaking, and organizing must be born anew out of this prayer and action.'[21] And the practical action he accordingly proposes is: 'The church is the church only when it exists for others. To make a start, it should give away all its property to those in need. The clergy must live solely on the free-will offerings of their congregations, or possibly engage in some secular calling. . . . it is not abstract argument, but example, that gives its word emphasis and power.'[22] Re-expressed in the tone of voice of revolutionary activism, we find any number of similar utterances at the present day, even to the point where the function of the sermon is transformed into the provocative anti-sermon.

We shall not stop to expose the weaknesses in these expressions of feeling and intention. In so far as such views are genuine and not in their turn mere verbalizing, talk about talk, the suffering expressed in them is provoked by a situation which is also our own. If we are conscious of this in such a way that we too suffer from it, then of course the breathless reiteration of the slogan 'deeds, not words', or the demagogic cry 'nothing but empty formulas' will bring us little relief. We can perhaps see most clearly, in the context of our quotations from Bonhoeffer, that boredom with words is merely the negative side of a longing for the true word: 'It is not for us to prophesy the day (though the day will come) when men will once more be called so to utter the word of God that the world will be changed and renewed by it. It will be a new language, perhaps quite non-religious, but liberating and redeeming – as was Jesus' language; it will shock people and yet overcome them by its power; it will be the language of a new righteousness and truth, proclaiming God's peace with men and the coming of his kingdom.'[23] This has the character of a testament, to which one does no justice by despising words. And even if forced to silence oneself, one could agree with Bonhoeffer only if the necessity for silence was tolerated unwillingly, and if the attempt was made, paradoxically, to give utterance to it, keeping a close look-out for fundamental experiences which could once again give rise to genuine and conscientious speech and reveal the possibility of making a wholesome and saving use of words.

This brings us close to something which, usually without any conscious connection with the range of problems faced by Christian language, has become one of the main themes of modern creative writing. This is that words fail and silence threatens, unless one succeeds in making at least the silence the theme of a creative utterance. In the form of a fictional letter from Lord Chandos to Francis Bacon, set in the early seventeenth century, Hugo von Hofmannsthal describes what at the beginning of the twentieth century he, but not he alone, experienced as a shattering crisis of language. Since then it has become a basic theme of modern literature (although often enough in an artificial and simulated form of expression). The letter is supposed to be one of apology to his friend 'for his total renunciation of literary activity'. Permit me to quote at length from this impressive poetic account of the failure of language.[24]

'My case, in short, is this. I have completely lost the ability to think or speak coherently about anything. At first it gradually became impossible for me to discuss any lofty or universal theme, or in so doing to utter the words of which all people make regular use without thinking about it. I felt an inexplicable discomfort merely in speaking words such as "spirit", "soul" or "body". I found it inwardly impossible to pass a judgment upon affairs of court, events in parliament, or what you will. And this was not out of any kind of discretion, for you know my frankness, which goes to the point of thoughtlessness. But the abstract words which the tongue is bound to use for these matters, in order to bring to light some kind of judgment, turned to dust in my mouth like rotten mushrooms.'[25] What is described first as a lack of assurance and then a total constraint in passing judgment on public matters, not for lack of courage, but because language, with its inevitable universality, was not fit for the task, suffered from a lack of substance, and as it were decomposed and fell apart, was now repeated in another, private sphere of speech. There it presented itself as the disappearance of the authority even to correct the lies of a child, because the words with which this could have been done themselves became insubstantial and powerless and were empty of the truth that should convince. 'It happened that I wanted to reprimand my four-year-old daughter Katharina Pompilia for a childish lie which she had told, and teach her the necessity of always being truthful. But as I tried the words that flowed into my mouth suddenly took on so fluctuating a colour, and became so entangled with one another, that I brought the sentence to an end as best I could. As if I had felt ill (in fact I was actually pale in the face), and striking my forehead violently, I left the child, closed the door behind me and only came to some degree back to my senses on horseback, after galloping a long way across the lonely common.'[26]

A third stage followed, in which even in everyday talk, the simplest subjects of conversation, he could no longer let himself be carried away by what was familiar; the power of speech failed him, because the right to speech had become wholly problematic. 'Gradually this impediment extended its range, like a spreading rust. Even in informal and casual conversation, all the judgments which I had been accustomed to make with the facility and the assurance of a sleep-walker became so open to question that I had to stop taking part in any such conversations. I was filled with inexplicable anger, which with difficulty and ill success I concealed, to hear such things as: "This matter turned out well or ill for such-and-such a person, Sheriff N. is a bad man, Preacher T. is a good man, Farmer M. is unfortunate, his sons are prodigals; someone else is to be envied because his daughters are thrifty; one family is on the way up, another is on the way down." All these statements seemed to me as far beyond proof, as lying and as terrible as ever they could be.'[27]

Let us pause here for a moment to look back and consider what this account of the crisis of language betrays about its causes. The text itself contains a warning against any attempt to clarify the matter. The incomprehensibility of the distress and anger is explicitly mentioned. It comes upon a person as strange transformation, a sudden malaise, a loss of the automatic security which he needs to live. He is defenceless against it, and can only describe with difficulty these experiences; 'these strange intellectual pains', the passage reads, 'this rapid springing of the branch with its fruit out of the reach of my hands, the drawing back of the murmuring water from my thirsty lips'.[28] Thus it is the pain of one who, the more he reaches out to take hold of what he longs for, the more he sees it vanish. And yet there are hints which contribute something to an understanding of what is happening. It is no accident that the three examples of the loss of speech concern judgments: judgments on public, moral and everyday matters. That is, statements which relate the concrete to the universal, understand it against a wider background and so as it were put it on trial and pass a judgment upon it. But this raises the question of the right to make such a judgment. What is it derived from? What justifies one in saying this or that? What is the basis of this kind of utterance? How can it be credible? These questions suddenly bear down with such force that the protective wall of what is customary and taken for granted can no longer resist them. General terms – which speech cannot do without, for it lives on generalizations – are discredited. The context which they represent and which ought to be their guarantee disappears. And thus even when speech is saying something true, it turns into a lie, because the question of its right to utterance drives it to silence.

Hofmannsthal's Lord Chandos describes this loss of speech, in the form of a loss of context, in terms of an uncanny proximity and bodily contact of the individual object, which, in its atomization, has become isolated from all concepts, and from every attempt to sum it up in speech. The atoms of speech, all that remain of language, the empty words, now produce not understanding but a strange alienation, and instead of offering you something, take hold of you like a whirlpool and carry you off into the void. 'My mind forced me to see all the things that came up in such a conversation in an uncanny proximity; just as once I saw a piece of the skin of my little finger in a magnifying glass, and it looked like a field with furrows and hollows, so I now perceived men and their actions. I no longer succeeded in apprehending them with the simplifying gaze of habit. Everything seemed to me to fall into fragments, the fragments into smaller fragments still, and nothing could any longer be grasped by a concept. The individual words swam round me; they came together in eyes which stared at me and into which I had to stare back: they were whirlpools which made me dizzy to gaze into, which turned without ceasing and which led down into the void.'[29]

But these negative, destructive aspects of the crisis of language are not all, although what follows does not provide an answer to them. Yet something eventually shines through the mystery of what speech really ought to be and could be. Of course there is no help to be found in language already spoken, traditional language, however classical. The attempt to find salvation in the intellectual world of antiquity is a failure. Lord Chandos has already given up hope of finding help in the lofty flights of Platonic thought. And likewise, the harmony of defined and ordered concepts in Seneca and Cicero – an aesthetic pleasure like a marvellous fountain with golden balls – has no room for the most profound and personal matters in his thinking. He feels shut out. Yet strangely enough the first step towards a change occurs at the very point where the atomization of reality brings about the atomization of language. In the mindless and thoughtless flow of everyday existence there are still joyful and inspiring moments.

What is the source of this unexpectedly moving, inwardly fulfilling and joyful power? And what has it to do with speech? Well, at first the only thing is that nothing is less capable of being summed up in words. 'It is not easy for me to tell you what these happy moments consist of; once again, I cannot find the words. For in truth it is something completely nameless, and it may well be almost unnameable, which at such moments, pouring into and filling some feature of my everyday surroundings with an overflowing flood of higher life, makes itself known to me.'[30] He must do what he can with examples, and asks indulgence in advance for their naïvety. 'A watering-can, a harrow left on the field, a dog in the sun, a neglected churchyard, a cripple, a small peasant cottage, any of these can be the vessel of my revelation. Each of these objects and the thousands like them, over which the eye would otherwise pass with indifference, taking them for granted, can suddenly take on for me at any moment, though it does not lie in my power to choose the moment, a noble and moving appearance, which I can find no words to express. Indeed, it can even be the clear recollection of an absent object which is incomprehensibly chosen to be filled to the brim with that gentle and suddenly rising flood of divine emotion.'[31] And this is substantiated by the account of the effect on him of the horrifying conception of the death struggles of poisoned rats. He was not seized by pity. 'It was something much more and much less than pity: an immense sympathy, a flowing over into those creatures or a feeling that a fluid of life and death, of dreaming and wakening had flowed over into them for a moment – where from?'[32] A similar feeling could be brought on by much more innocent causes, such as the sight of a water-beetle swimming from one side to the other of the dark surface of the water in a watering-can.

What is the point of these joyful and inspiring moments? This can only be expressed by the shocking contrast that the most insignificant and even horrible things can be the source of splendour and happiness. 'In these moments a creature of no significance, a dog, a rat, a beetle, a stunted apple tree, a cart track winding across the hillside, a moss-covered stone could be more to me than the most beautiful and submissive lover on the most joyful night there has ever been. These dumb and some-times inanimate creatures come up to meet me with such a fullness, such a presence of love, that my delighted eye is actually incapable of falling upon a single dead spot round about them. Everything, everything there is, everything I can recall, everything that my most confused thoughts touch on, seems to me to be something.'[33]

Let us try once again to sum up and understand what is being described here. One has no more control over this experience than one has any defence against the onset of the crisis of language. But by contrast to that shattering experience of utter emptiness, it brings a joyful tremor of overflowing fullness. It signifies not one's doom, but rather that one has been specially chosen. It can be most accurately described as an experience of presence, of the fullest, most sublime presence, the presence of the infinite, the presence of love. It can be described in numerous ways. But presence is the opposite of the distance which is characteristic of the universal, of concepts and relationships. These slip away from anyone who approaches them and tries to take hold of them. Presence is life itself, indeed a higher divine life, experienced as present, even when it occurs in the form of a dying rat. Presence as such is the delightful, superabundant, joyful experience of love.

Does this mean that it is the direct opposite of speech? Is it a kind of renunciation of the word? The statements about this are strangely ambiguous. But it is certainly a matter of a direct experience, unmediated by speech, of the unobtrusive, 'and its lying or standing around, unobserved by anyone, its unspeaking being, can become the source of this enigmatic, wordless, limitless delight'.[34]

But this process without words hints at what words could do if they were available, and it arouses a longing for the possibility of uttering what has been experienced. 'This combination of objects without significance', we read, 'sent through me a feeling of such a presence of the infinite', 'from the roots of the hair down to the marrow of the heel', 'that I should like to break out into words, words which, if I could find them, I know would bring down to earth those cherubim, in which I do not believe . . .'[35] For it is not a matter of an unconscious ecstasy, nor of forgetfulness of the world in a mindless torpor. For these joyful and life-giving moments are understood as the miraculous points of light which stand out from normal uncomprehending and unthinking existence. Not only does the individual thing, the presence of which is suddenly borne in on one, now appear as a reality for the first time; as such, it also enables everything that exists to appear as a reality. That is, it is a presence which makes reality present.

Here an opening towards the whole of existence takes place on a wide scale. A perceptibly wider horizon comes into view, and thinking of a comprehensive kind takes place, albeit thinking of a different kind from that of reason: thinking with the heart. Once again we quote in full what we have para-phrased: 'Even my own dullness, the usual torpor of my brain, seems to me to be a reality. I feel in and round me a delightful and completely infinite play of contraries, and amongst the conflicting substances there is none into which I may not flow. It seems to me then as if my body consists of nothing but ciphers, which reveal everything to me. Or as if we could enter into a new, mysterious relationship to the whole of existence if we begin to think with the heart. But when this strange enchantment passes from me, I am not able to say anything about it. I could no more describe in rational words the nature of this harmony which pours through me and the whole world, and how it makes itself perceptible to me, than I could give details of the inner movement of my intestines or the blockages of my bloodstream.'[36] Thus it is a kind of thought that does not simply exclude speech, but calls for speech of a special kind, a speech which unlike the provincial dialects of ordinary people is a universal language, because it is the language of things themselves. Of this way of thinking, which seems utterly foolish the moment anyone tries to express it in words, we read that it 'is a kind of feverish thought, but thought conducted in a material which is more direct, more fluent and more intense than words. There are also whirlpools, but unlike the whirlpools of language they do not seem to lead into the bottomless void, but in some way into myself and into the deepest womb of peace.'[37] So Lord Chandos is convinced that he will no longer write another book in English or in Latin, 'because the language which would perhaps be given to me not only to write in, but also to think in, is neither Latin nor English nor Italian nor Spanish, but a language the words of which are not even known to me, a language in which dumb things speak to me and of which I shall perhaps some day have to give an account in the grave to an unknown judge.'[38]

It may be thought paradoxical – and yet it is perhaps the expression of a simple truth – that the consciousness of a profound crisis of language, and indeed a complete collapse of language, has produced a text in language of unusual force and power of expression. The explanation of the reason for silence, as it were the farewell letter to the literary use of language, makes the impression of an unusually fine literary achievement, precisely because it displays the opposite of what it asserts, the power of language and the courage to use it. In my view there is no contradiction here. The greatest achievements of language will always be when it struggles with what is beyond words. And the experience of the failure of language leads to the apprehension of a true language, transcending all the existing possibilities of language. To what is expressed in this poetic passage about, and by means of, the compulsion to be silent, one might apply the biblical verse which says that only the time of trial teaches one to pay attention to the word.[39] Of course one must not turn the ideas in this passage of creative literature into the manifesto of a philosophy of language. To give an adequate explanation of the questions raised here would not only mean enlarging on them and making them more precise, but would also call for considerable criticism. For one can hardly be satisfied with this view of language and words.

Nevertheless, it is a very impressive presentation of two insights which must be taken into account in setting out to produce a theological theory of language. The first concerns the cause of the crisis of language. It lies in the fact that the coherent structure of understanding has broken down, because language has taken on an existence of its own and has become isolated from its basis in experience. Consequently the words are uttered into a void, their universality becomes universality and nothing more. They are no longer in touch with the concrete and treat it as hostile.

The question which shows whether or not language is genuine, and which in any particular case can reveal concealed crises of language to good effect, is the question of the credibility of what is uttered, of its basis, of its justification and vindication. The other insight, which concerns the origin of language, is closely related to this. The experience of a presence which makes reality present sets language free again. 'Out of the abundance of the heart the mouth speaks.'[40] This seems to contradict the text we have been commenting on, for it states that the experience of presence cannot be uttered in speech. But we must remember that there is a difference between a failure of language because one is empty and has nothing to say, and a failure of language because one is too full of what compels one to speak. Now if a genuine and original use is made of language, it is always true that giving birth to speech cannot be done without pain, any more than giving birth to a child. Thomas Mann once said that an author was a person who found writing particularly difficult.[41] Even if one's mouth literally overflows and the heart pours itself out in language, it will rarely be without pain at the fact that at such a time, perhaps then above all, what is said falls far short of what is there to be said. But the reverse can be true: a single word can be of an infinite and inexhaustible power of utterance and fill the whole heart, as Luther was aware.[42] Thus we can find in Hofmannsthal's text a pointer towards the overcoming of the crisis of language. That is, one must not shut oneself off from the experience of the presence which makes reality present – though of course one must be aware that it is something completely beyond one's own control.

An important task for a theological theory of language is to study the phenomenon of boredom with language in a comprehensive analysis of all the different areas of present-day life: its causes and symptoms, the things that conceal it and compensate for it, the suffering it causes and also the grounds it gives for hope – which are not altogether absent. The 'Letter of Lord Chandos' can to some extent be regarded as representative of the crisis of language in our age, although it presents it in only a partial fashion, and not in all its variety – which is not to detract from the brilliance of this text – nor in all its profundity. By discussing it at such length we have at least emphasized by an impressive example the fact that what may seem to be a highly specialized concern with a theological theory of language confronts us directly with the sphinx-like countenance of our age.

I must limit myself to a cursory note on the range of phenomena which fall within the field we are considering. Modern literature is a unique struggle, in the midst of a general experience of the loss of language and the wearing out of language, of a distaste for stereotyped patterns of speech and cheap hand-me-down language, to return to genuine statements, credible words, and a conscientious use of language. Of course the greater part of its attempts fall short of this lofty claim. And it is readily comprehensible that even where writing shows high quality, it often carries repulsive marks of the struggle, and in its fragmentary, tortured language provides more evidence of the decay of language than it offers help in reconstructing it. But it is a moving fact, that in an age which seems to concentrate exclusively on obtaining technological control over the world, there is a powerful and basic need to grope towards the intangible in language, to sum up one's own experience in words, and as it were to set up refuges of language to which the people of our age can take flight.

All around us we find a use of language which may well arouse in us the fear that we are being smothered. Consider the use of language in politics and economics, and the thousand possibilities of manipulation, not only with the aid of language, but even of language itself. In propaganda and advertising it has become an instrument of power of the first rank, and yet, in this most effective form, it is the cause of a rapid loss of speech and the disappearance of confidence in language. One no longer expects of the word that one can rely upon it, that one can take it at its word. The experience is that language is no longer any use for what it is really meant to do, and what it alone can do, that is, to make possible understanding, to bring assent, to establish peace, to arouse confidence and to give freedom. Rather, it permits itself to be misused with startling success to achieve the very opposite. In view of this cynical use of language it is understandable that people take refuge in a kind of minimum use of language, limiting themselves to a language which is free of error, but for that reason aseptic and sterile. It excludes on principle any possibility of mis-understanding, and is a language of purely statistical information, formalized into a calculus so that one can use it to compute without snags and absolutely accurately, and is excused by it from any need for reflection. Of course the language of everyday discourse remains indispensable in spite of this. But it is subject to a continuous shrinking process and is becoming sketchy and lacking in expression. There are tangible difficulties of language which affect our personal dealings with one another. Apart from technical information, it is scarcely possible to say anything of essential significance, and perhaps we even have nothing more to say. A real letter, in which the writer gives something of himself, is becoming a rarity, and if someone succeeds in writing such a letter and in doing so causes happiness, it is felt to be a miracle. In all of these examples anyone can find enough that applies to himself to make him reflect upon the crisis of language at the present day.

CHAPTER II

The Jungle of the Problem
of Language

In dealing with the theme of 'language' one nowadays finds oneself faced with a discouraging mass of literature. One of the characteristics of our age is academic overproduction, and not even the relevant specialists can adequately acquaint themselves with all that appears, and make use of it. Together with the constant advance of specialization, it hinders rather than helps communication. In the nature of things the amount of research and discussion papers reaches record level in any field in which the interests of very different academic disciplines meet, overlap and compete. This has happened in the case of the problem of language, which is nowadays an immediate issue to a surprising extent. It is the focus of interest in the most widely differing fields. Philosophical tendencies concerned predominantly with the history of thought, or with mathematics and the natural sciences; fields of study concerned with language in the narrower sense, be it with literature or semantics and linguistics; psychology and behavioural studies, ethnology and sociology; or, to mention the two subjects of the whole range which are most remote from each other, theology and technology, with their characteristic conceptions of cybernetics (for 'cybernetics' was once the name of a theological discipline!), represented on the one hand by the word of mouth of witnesses and on the other hand by the calculations carried out by a computer: all these find themselves drawn into the whirlpool of debate on the theory of language. But in spite of an astonishing degree of similarity in the themes they discuss there is not, on the whole, a corresponding exchange of ideas between disciplines, for the phenomena and aspects of the problem which they study are usually a very one-sided selection.

As far as theology is concerned, one should not try to make a virtue of necessity and retreat to a situation where theology plays the role of a mere outsider in this common preoccupation with the theory of language. It would at first sight be very easy to isolate theology from the rest and, seeking additional justification from the tendency to specialize, to concern oneself with theology alone. But to do so would be to throw away at once everything that is to be gained from a theological theory of language: that is, an escape from the damaging isolation of theology and responsible use of theological language in contact with the general awareness of language.

Not merely because the situation seems confused, however, is it appropriate to speak of 'the jungle of the problem of language'. Behind direct and urgent pressure of the difficulties raised by the present state of academic research, specific practical problems are mounting up. The innumerable ways in which these problems are entangled and intertwined with language is something we must consider at least in brief outline.

I. LANGUAGE AND LANGUAGES

The great risk of the subdivision of the object of our study into an immeasurable multitude of separate problems can be seen at once from the fact that it is so difficult to justify speaking of 'language'. Of course one cannot just drop the use of the term in the singular. It sums up in one word everything that belongs to the phenomenon of language, and is no doubt expressing more than an empty general concept, summing up the multitude of languages in a single abstract entity. But what is it that embraces and unites all languages? The nature of the problem only appears when we realize the numerous points of view from which one can speak of a multitude of different languages.

The first obvious one is that of the number of different languages and dialects spoken in the world; it runs into thousands. Notwithstanding its relationships with others, each of these languages is self-sufficient in that on principle it includes the whole of what can be said. Man is normally monoglot. He speaks his mother tongue; he learnt to speak by learning to speak that language. It is usually adequate as a medium of speech for understanding and mutual assent. Consequently, to learn other languages is a basically different process, because one is no longer learning simply to speak, but to understand and speak another language on the basis of an ability to deal with language which has already been acquired. For this reason a second language which a person has learnt can hardly ever replace his mother tongue.

This makes clear the way in which different vernaculars, and the different colloquial languages, are related to each other. They can be translated into one another but not replaced by one another. And this irreplaceability is by no means merely subjective in nature, as if only a lack of practice were the reason why a person's mother tongue has almost always undisputed primacy. Rather, what we find here is an intrinsic limit to the possibility of translating languages at all. No translation can replace the original. And the more original the language of the translated version, the more unsuccessful the translation of the original. For every language has its own power of expression, which can only imperfectly be reproduced in a translation. There are many reasons for this, such as – to mention only the most obvious – the greatly varying nuances of meaning in vocabulary and the differing forms of accidence and syntax. A translation is of course even harder when what is actually said is the vehicle of unspoken and inexpressible meaning, referring to matters which convey general impressions of the most elementary but most profound kind, and so are inextricably linked with the characteristic feelings and perceptions of human beings. Thus, for example, the translation of lyric poetry brings with it the most acute experience of the difficulties and limits of a translation. Thus the learning of foreign languages is by no means restricted to the technical ability to make use, in spite of linguistic differences, of the possibilities of mutual understanding and assent which they offer. Rather, it means coming into possession of something of what is irreplaceable, because it is untranslatable, in a particular language, and so enriching and enlarging one's own linguistic horizon.

I refer to these well-known facts because they emphasize how rich and instructive an example of the historical nature of man the phenomenon of language is. The vast number of languages shows how thoroughly the field of history is subdivided. It reminds us of the great influence on history of linguistic units, although they are by no means necessarily identical with political units. With the aim of overcoming sources of historical tension, as the universalization of the course of history proceeds, the creation of a unified world language might seem attractive. A universal language which all men had as their mother tongue – and not until this was achieved would the linguistic unity of mankind be a reality – is of course out of the question for the foreseeable future, and may perhaps always be a Utopian ideal. But quite apart from the prospects of success, there is reason to fear that the loss of the variety of languages would result in an immense loss of richness of life and humanity.

But the great variety of vernaculars is only one aspect, the linguistic aspect, of the many different facets under which language presents itself to us. Within one and the same language, in the linguistic sense, very different languages can exist. Part of their vocabulary may be peculiar to themselves, or they may make a characteristic choice of words, and perhaps even possess special grammatical rules. In any case they will display typical turns of phrase. The many possible forms which such language can take can be summed up as those of group languages and specialist languages.

The first case is that in which individual social groups express their distinctive nature in certain forms of speech, and so protect it. That is, they enhance the feeling of union and concord within the group itself by the use of a language with which the outsider is not immediately familiar, and which makes him emphatically aware of the fact that he does not belong. Examples of this are the language of royal courts or the language of academic solemnities or – to avoid giving the impression that these are all obsolescent cases – private-school slang, soldiers' slang, or the language of particular parties or sects. One might well consider under what circumstances Christian language becomes such a group language. Certainly a church language which takes some particular form, or the language of particular parties in the Church, must be included in this category.

In the case of specialist languages it is a matter of the deliberate standardization of usage, and the giving of technical meanings to words, in order to simplify and ensure understanding by means of a standard terminology. Whereas these specialist languages show marked differences from the language of every-day usage and are only coloured by it incidentally, the group languages mentioned above are in every sense forms of every-day language, although often specifically restricted to a certain situation in life, or to speaking to certain persons. Basically, technical languages are not suitable for translation. At the very least they lose their precision and therefore the quality of their statement if they are transferred into the language of general everyday usage. That is why in those sciences which are not closely related to history there is a prevailing tendency to use an international vocabulary, if not a language of mathematical formulae utterly remote from the language of everyday discourse. Group languages are translatable in theory. Yet they are either intended to make translation as difficult as possible, in order to preserve their esoteric character – thieves' cant is an example of this – or else they are in theory interested in translation, but have difficulty about this because of the danger of the loss of the group's identity – for example, a political party, seeking to publicize its views, which is held together by the use of a particular ideological jargon. Church history also offers examples of both cases. Of course the boundary between group languages and specialist languages is a fluid one, in so far as groups are constituted by a narrow interest in a particular matter, or the commitment of specialists to a particular task leads to the formation of groups.

One might also consider whether, in addition to the above-mentioned categories, one should also introduce the point of view of ontological differences between languages. What I mean is this. A language can be marked throughout by the understanding of reality which is dominant in it. The language of the magical understanding of reality is different from that of the mythical understanding, the metaphysical understanding, or the scientific understanding in the modern sense. Or think again of the very different understandings of reality which have been as it were crystallized in the structures of particular languages. The differences between Hebrew and Greek are a particularly significant example of this, though they demand a very cautious and circumspect assessment of the differences. One might also refer to the languages of primitive people, in which very surprising and yet very instructive ways of understanding reality find expression. From Wilhelm von Humboldt down to structuralism, they have always had a particularly stimulating effect upon the study of the theory of language.

The numerous instances of overlapping which occur in such an attempt to classify languages make it very difficult to say what justifies the claim to be called a 'language'. However unsatisfactory it may be to restrict oneself to a purely linguistic definition of a language as a unit, to go beyond this to a use of the word 'language' which cuts across linguistic subdivisions can easily reduce everything to confusion. The danger is even greater when the use of the word 'language' actually goes outside the linguistic sphere, and people talk of such things as the language of bees or the language of material things, the language of facts, the language of the heart, the language of gestures, the language of the body, and so forth. Such expressions cannot of course simply be dismissed as purely metaphorical. For they have a bearing on understanding, and in a strict sense this is the proper function and responsibility of language as a linguistic phenomenon. But the range of understanding is too wide for it to be conveyed exclusively by linguistic forms and utterances. And indeed this extra means of expression is by no means something additional to and distinct from language in a strict sense. The different threads are woven together here in a particularly dense texture. Only by means of spoken language is it possible to listen to a language which transcends spoken language, such as the language of the heart or that of facts; and spoken language is itself dependent upon the fact that the range of the phenomenon of language goes further than it does itself. When one is dealing with language, one is necessarily dealing with more than language in the narrow sense, expressed in sounds or legible signs and summarized in grammatical rules.

Thus one must not force an artificial precision and clarity upon the word by artificially restricting its meaning. This would be to curtail and impoverish it. In my view it is doubtful whether Wittgenstein's concept of language as a game is adequate to do justice to the complexity of language, in so far as it is dominated by a tendency to isolate language games, like monads, from each other. It overestimates the numerous varieties at the expense of the way they interpenetrate each other. For it is characteristic of the phenomenon of language that the different concrete forms it takes are accessible one to another, and actually make the attempt to pass from one language into another. Communication is so closely linked with the phenomenon of language that not only is there communication within each individual language, but a process of communication also takes place between languages. The fact that there are limits to this (as indeed to communication within the field of a single language) is something that lies in the nature of any understanding. For understanding always extends to the refractory nature of what is incommunicable. If, in spite of this, one can speak of a full and unlimited understanding in the relationship between one person and another, and this expression is not to be considered a mere hyperbole, then the justification for it lies in a comprehensive account of understanding which includes even what is incommunicable.

2. POLARITIES IN LANGUAGE AS A LIVING PROCESS

The jungle of the problem of language is not merely a product of the great multitude and variety of *languages*, which ultimately makes it difficult to say what deserves to be called a language at all. We are also faced with a confusing abundance of *ways of looking at language*. They do not come into existence fortuitously, but neither are they merely linked to various types of language. Rather, they reflect in various facets the situation, extraordinarily complex and difficult to define, in which one finds oneself when one reflects about language. It is clearly inadequate to tie language down to an objective definition based on a technical system of signs and rules, similar to the moves and rules of chess. To restrict oneself to the way language is presented in dictionaries and grammars, which at first sight present a complete inventory of it, does not do justice to the wide-ranging phenomenon of language. Language must be sought out where it is used and experienced as a living utterance and a necessity of life. When this is done, a number of polarities come to light, making it clear that language is not something isolated in itself, but takes place as a living process.

a. Potentiality and Act

Of course there is some truth in the naïve and objectivizing conception of language as a system which can be used as a complicated instrument, capable of infinite modulation, as though one were playing on an organ which had a range of notes, stops, keyboards and pedals, which offered an infinite series of combinations. It would show a poor understanding of how language can be used (even one's own mother tongue), if dictionaries were not valued as treasuries of the riches of language and grammars as an aid to the correct use of language. Language undoubtedly contains, ready for use, an inexhaustible supply of linguistic material, of which any individual only ever requires a tiny portion in his own use of language. Between the language one uses and its actual application, between its passive and its active use, between the range of language one can understand and the extent of what one utters oneself, there is always a great gulf. But it would be inadequate to base a concept of language solely on the potentiality of language, and to regard every concrete use of language merely as the application of language to discourse and conversation – as though the concrete use contributed nothing to the understanding of language as such. To divide language in this way into potentiality and act, allocating everything which we understand by language exclusively to the former extreme of the polarity, falls down in the face of the fact that even as a pure instrument language is not a fixed entity, complete in itself.

Language is historical through and through. It betrays its origin to anyone who is attentive to his own use of it by the numerous indications of etymology, semantic history or idiom, just as a tree reveals its age by its annual rings. Language is never complete. As long as it lives it is moving, changing. Parts of it grow obsolete and die out, and innovations grow up to replace them. And this, the life of language, takes place only in its actual use. Dictionaries and grammars are no more than secondary abstractions and interpretations of a situation which, as the concrete use of language, is prior to every reduction of language to a system with formal rules. Of course there are innumerable occasions for using the established rules to avoid errors, solecisms and the decay of language. But seen as a whole, even the most perfect distillation of a language into vocabulary and grammar must ultimately concede victory to a development of language which goes beyond the ideal of the purity of a language which was valid at a particular time, and which may quite often even legitimize what were once errors. This is a sign that the living and concrete use of language ultimately has priority, and even exercises a normative function upon language as a formalized and fixed instrumental system.

But a one-sided emphasis upon a single aspect of the phenomenon of language should not be resisted by equally unbalanced emphasis on the opposite aspect. Anyone who is interested in the problem of language from the philosophical or theological point of view is usually faced with a difficulty, scarcely to be overestimated, in the fact that he cannot ignore questions of linguistics and the history of language; and yet a non-specialist is scarcely capable of doing justice to them. A lack of thorough knowledge and the appropriate skills in these highly specialized fields of scholarship can all too easily lead to speculative constructions. Scarcely anyone can make a statement upon the problem of language, in any sense which takes into account the whole range of issues involved, without the reservation that he is aware of the considerable gaps in his own technical knowledge and the degree to which his arguments are subject to correction. But this admission ought not to prevent anyone from emphasizing the phenomena to which he has learnt to pay particular attention from his own point of view and within the horizon of his own experience. What is the event of language ultimately concerned with? What is it that makes man ultimately dependent upon language? How do the utterances of language come into being at all, and how do they achieve their aim? What hampers understanding or even makes it impossible? What are the conditions for the utterances of language to be understood? How far is this affected by the situation in which the event of language takes place? What is achieved by language and by language alone? The study of what is at issue in language depends of course upon numerous branches of special research. But it does justice to its task only if it goes on to the large question of what it is to be human and the relation of humanity to reality. We shall make this clear by examining further polarities.

b. The Community and the Individual

It is no accident that the situation of language provides perhaps what is the best model for making clear the relationship between the community and the individual. It can also be a guide in correcting distorted concepts of this relationship. Language is of its nature something common, something social. It would be absurd for everyone to create and speak his own language. The result of this would be to bring language to an end. For by language the individual is drawn into the life of the community, and in this way above all he first takes shape as a human being. To see the fundamental process by which someone becomes a human being through learning to speak is a constant astonishment. Here we shall do no more than point to a few of its main features.

The ability to learn to speak and to handle language is of course given to man as an inherited characteristic. But language itself is not a biological inheritance. It must be acquired and is imparted – in complete isolation from heredity – by the environment in which the child is placed. A child could on principle learn any other language as its mother tongue, just as easily and naturally. With regard to the fundamental process of learning to speak at all, language is only imparted by others speaking to you. Thus language is imparted only by language. Teaching someone to speak and learning to speak is the most fundamental of all acts of communication through language. In some respects this is the most extreme and most astonishing achievement of which language is capable; it is as it were the act by which the community of language is begotten. But what results from this in terms of language is by no means merely the narrow community of language between mother and child. Of course this elementary I-thou relationship, and with it love in its most immediate and natural form, comes first. It forms as it were the gateway to language. But through this gateway there is access into the infinite spaces of the community which is created by language: with people distant and far away, with contemporaries and with previous generations, those of the past who become present through language.

Language contains within itself the whole fullness (and paradoxically this also includes the whole poverty) of the life and suffering of the human race. The experience of the world and the experiences of the mystery of reality are present in it. Every new arrival amongst men partakes through language in what mankind has learnt long before his time and in what mankind has produced. Thanks to language, the newborn child does not begin at the very starting point of history, but at *his own* place within the *whole continuity* of history. If there were any need of proof of how utterly man is rooted in mankind, of which he is a member, one need only pause at the fact of language and think about it. This is a precaution against a view of man which isolates him as an individual being, and against a non-historical attitude which can be adopted only as a form of self-deception.

But it is obvious that the other pole also has its place. Language can be spoken only by an individual. Only the 'I' can speak. And a person has only learned to speak if he can use language with his own choice of words for which he himself is responsible. And this forms a focal point for what is characteristic of the life of a human being: how he uses the right of participation to which the possession of speech entitles him, and which it also accords to him. This personal responsibility in using language, which is of the nature of personality, must not be confused with a creative originality of language, which of course is rare. But those at least who in some respect bear public responsibility for language have an obligation to devote themselves to the activity of language in such a way that they share in forming and shaping language, and, within the limits in which this is meaningful, actually speak a language of their own. But neither these genuinely exceptional cases, nor the pretentious attempts to create artificially and to simulate what is only genuine as a gift received, should divert our attention from the personal responsibility, quite different in nature, which is laid on everyone who uses language.

Of course the use that man makes of speech is in general imitative. His way of expressing himself shows where he gets it from. He speaks the language of his time, or of a particular language tradition in which he stands. For the most part he simply uses the usual turns of phrase which lie at hand, ready for every possible occasion. In a strange anonymous process of continuous linguistic change they are reproduced and laid out ready for use by the forces which shape language over time, or, as the German phrase has it, *durch den Volksmund*, 'by the mouth of the people'. They appear as proverbs, as set patterns of speech, as fashionable colloquialisms or as slang. It is possible to observe in oneself how much one simply repeats what has been said before, confines oneself to narrow limits of language and speaks the way everybody else speaks. We need not go on to discuss the corruptions of the use of language which occur in vast numbers as the result of carelessness and a lack of conscientiousness. It is all too easy to overlook the other side of this. Even the normal, wholesome use of language includes a large amount of ready-made language, of language off the shelf. Set forms such as the different ways of addressing people, the phrases of everyday conversation, or the ways in which one reacts in words to certain experiences of life by way of congratulation or condolence, the way one encourages people or cheers them up; all this can be valuable, giving real support and stability to life. This is not something that should be underestimated or despised. Of course the social function of conventions, of the well-practised traffic regulations of language, is limited in its justification and necessity. A study of this would bring a rich harvest of observations in the sociology of language. But even when one takes careful account of all these ways in which language is derivative and conditioned, and by means of which the use of language largely takes place, or even almost exclusively for most people, this is not enough to remove the initiative of the individual with regard to language. Rather, *within* all these derivative forms, the responsibility of the individual for language becomes acute.

This responsibility is expressed less in the *form* of language, which in most cases is conventional, than in the apprehension of the *situation* of language and in the way justice is done to it. Here too there is a wide field for observations at which we can do no more than hint. The very moment at which a person chooses to speak or to keep his silence, whom he allows to speak to him and whom he refuses, show how much he possesses or lacks a responsibility for language. (Of course he can display both either by speaking or by keeping silent.) Even when it is a question merely of joining in with what other people say it is important to whom he listens, in what he joins in, to whom he lends his voice, and to whose advantage he makes use of his right to speak. And even when the statistics of the content of statements show them to be concerned with matters of little importance, not with profound insights but with everyday information, far more takes place by way of them than a grammatical analysis of the sentences would bring to light. For a person to say just this in this particular situation, to this particular person, can mean that he is not simply telling him what his words say, but through them is giving himself in a certain sense. When someone promises something or promises nothing, when someone gives his word, takes responsibility for something and is prepared to justify something, his statements point to the very essence of what it means for man to use language. Without these phenomena, language would literally have no life in it. The relationship of language to the situation in which it is uttered means that in and through language the speaker is irreplaceably present and answerable. One can see this simply by listing some of the many words and phrases which language itself possesses for defining the act of speaking on the basis of its relationship to its situation. That is, they are words which take into account what happens when language is used; for example: to ask, to complain, to mock, to teach, to exhort, to comfort, to insult, to blame, to acknowledge, to praise, etc.

c. Identity and Difference

Closely related to the polarity of the community and the individual is another tension within what takes place in language. On the one hand language is the essence of what men share and what joins them together. It brings understanding as a first step towards the mutual assent it aims to achieve. Heidegger's description of language as the 'house of being'[43] of course implies much more than our reflections at this point.

But it does express very effectively the security, the feeling of being at home, which is created by the familiar language in which one has grown up from childhood. Anyone who has spent a long time in a place where a foreign language is spoken knows what it means suddenly to hear his own language again and to be able to speak it. Once more you can say everything you want in a much more precise, subtle and intense way, and people understand you with less trouble and more directly. You can say much more with fewer words, and often mere allusions are enough, because you can rely upon a whole range of undertones and overtones of language. It is well known how difficult it is to understand a joke in a foreign language or even more to make a deliberate joke in a foreign language (of course you make any number of involuntary ones). Another linguistic contrast which can be experienced is this: Anyone who in some sort of official situation – on administrative committees, in court, or anywhere else – has had to use an official business language for any length of time feels able to breathe again when he can use a more intimate language in a familiar circle. He does not have to struggle to achieve understanding and assent and to overcome distrust. He is already understood, and can rely upon this and express himself, saying what is in his heart.

On the other hand of course, a common language is no guarantee of understanding. Often enough, it is only a common language which brings disagreements violently to a head. When participants whose background of language and ideas is very different meet in ecumenical dialogues, a very friendly atmosphere is established quickly under the deceptive appearance of agreement, because people are pleased to understand something of what the others are saying and are quite incapable of making themselves understood with regard to the real points of disagreement. It requires a great deal in common to make people aware at all of profound disagreements and to argue them out in discussions. The denominational disagreement between Catholics and Protestants in theological controversy has for example never been disputed so bitterly and stubbornly as in the period when both sides spoke the same language of baroque scholastic metaphysics. Both sides were convinced that they accurately understood the points of disagreement. It nowadays seems to us questionable whether this was really the case. For it is possible to argue at cross-purposes not only when you are speaking different languages, but even when you are speaking the same language. But in this case it must be said that, even and indeed especially when people are speaking the same language in an approximate sense, it may well be that they are speaking quite different languages.

This brings us to a characteristic ambivalence of language. On the one hand it brings immediate understanding as a first step. Anyone who has command of a language, and is at home in it, understands it without difficulty. It normally causes him no problems of mutual understanding and of assent. He makes use of it in so natural a way that he does not notice the highly complicated process which is taking place. We take as little notice of our own language as of the air we breathe or of our bodily functions when we are healthy. On the other hand, it is the task of language to mediate understanding and achieve assent; that is, to fight against the constant flaring up of incomprehension and misunderstanding, and to overcome the resistances with which it is faced. And the ambivalence of the situation is particularly prominent in the fact that language is not only the means by which understanding is achieved, but can also be the cause of a lack of understanding and misunderstanding, and can even be used deliberately to create misunderstandings, to deceive, and to lead into error. Thus language does not merely create community, it can also destroy it. The first step into the kingdom of truth is made possible by language, but so is the first step into the kingdom of lies. The Letter of James described the human tongue as an organ of speech which has a double tongue: 'With it we bless the Lord and Father, and with it we curse men, who are made in the likeness of God. From the same mouth come blessing and cursing.'[44]

The immediate conclusion to be drawn seems obvious: that language is a purely formal and neutral entity, and that consequently it is quite wrong to include this ambivalence in a discussion of the problem of language. And one could find in the many ways in which colloquial language is misused in practice a reason for regarding it with distrust, because of this ambiguity. This would lead to the demand for a rigorous formalization and neutralization of language, reducing it as far as possible to a usage which excludes every source of obscurity and allows only statements which are without question unequivocal. But the Letter of James takes a different course. By pointing out that the human tongue is double-tongued, it increases our awareness of the power of language and our consciousness of the responsibility for language. Language can do such serious harm only because, however unimportant it may seem to be, it plays a decisive part in making man what he is. 'If anyone makes no mistakes in what he says he is a perfect man, able to bridle the whole body also. If we put bits into the mouths of horses that they may obey us, we guide their whole bodies. Look at the ships also; though they are so great and are driven by strong winds, they are guided by a very small rudder wherever the will of the pilot directs.'[45]

There can be no doubt, then, that the theme of language is human existence as a whole. Thus the problem of language cannot be neutralized. Instead, it must be related to the fact that language shows what it is to be a human being and in what man's perfection consists. This stresses the great importance of language, but does not protect it from an abuse which is catastrophic in its effects precisely because language is so powerful and important. 'So the tongue is a little member and boasts of great things. How great a forest is set ablaze by a small fire! And the tongue is a fire. The tongue is an unrighteous world among our members, staining the whole body, setting on fire the cycle of nature, and set on fire by hell.'[46] In this perspective, the problem of language is concentrated upon the question of how language can be used in a saving and wholesome way. The power of language over man, for good and for evil, leads to the question of man's power over language. And here there is a difficulty which seems to lead to an impasse: 'For every kind of beast and bird, of reptile and sea creature, can be tamed and has been tamed by humankind, but no human being can tame the tongue – a restless evil, full of deadly poison.'[47]

At all events, this view of things does not regard the discipline of restricting language to logical operations as adequate to cope with the harm language can do. Of course an unequivocal use of language can be achieved by violent means, if the realm of ambivalence is avoided altogether; or else, since it is not practical to avoid it in colloquial language, if one can acquiesce in it as a fact of life, and cultivate in addition a technically perfect language, completely flawless, for particular scientific or scholarly purposes. But the passage in the Letter of James is concerned with a different way of avoiding ambivalence. It calls for language to be true, and for this to be fought for in the field of tension of this ambivalence itself. This clearly raises the question of how language ultimately comes to be uttered as concrete speech. What drives, inspires, and empowers people to speak, and what makes them speak in such a way as to make a good and wholesome use of language? Here the theological dimension of the problem of language is obviously raised. Two questions are posed: What part does the heart of man play in regard to language? And how far can speaking of God turn the powerlessness of man with regard to language into the power and authority to use it?

d. Language and its Subject

Before we go further in this direction, we must first turn to another polarity, that of language and its subject. The naïve view represents this relationship as a reflection in which that which is seen in the mirror corresponds exactly to what is looking into it. Of course it recognizes that the individual word is not a true image, but a mere cipher, a sign, which represents what it signifies, either by an audible sign or a written sign. There is some justification for this view of the function of language as a sign, but it is very limited. Individual words have a range of meaning which is greater or less in extent. They are not firmly attached to individual things like identity discs. They can include a variety of phenomena, sum up individual objects in complexes and act as general terms. This in itself introduces complications, which the sign theory of language must take into account by concept of the sign characterized by considerable variation in the degree to which the meaning of the sign depends upon the context. The attempt may nevertheless be made to deal with the complicated structure of language in strict accordance with the sign theory and to describe it with appropriate precision. That is, meanings are defined in such a way that no free play of meaning is allowed. If this attempt succeeds, the consequence is that language is no longer the occasion of misunderstanding; but it is also incapable of saying anything essential and never provokes thought. For the very openness of language to the influence of the context assumes that the hearer can exercise understanding as an intellectual act carried out by himself. That is, in order to understand what is said to him he is required to do something on his own account. It is this which makes the conveying of information in language genuinely fruitful.

The problems raised by the purely significative understanding of language become really difficult as soon as one turns from individual words and their relationship with things, to the sentence and its relationship with particular complex situations. The idea that language is primarily descriptive in character leads of itself, when it is closely examined, beyond the theory of language as a sign and image. For there is a fundamental distinction between the description and what is described. The description dissects the total situation, selects from it what is important in it, and fixes it, by means of the order of the words and the structure of the sentence, into the consecutive utterance typical of language. But the course taken by the event described is not identical with the order it follows within the sentence. This consideration draws our attention to the dominating significance of time for language, from two points of view. First of all, as an act, language always takes place consecutively in time, with the elements of speech following one another. It is no mere chance that the vehicle of expression in language is sound, which is transitory; it takes up time but fails rapidly with time. Secondly, the syntactical structure of a sentence is also necessarily determined by time. This leads us to the recognition that the basic model of utterances in language is not the description of situations in which time is of no concern, but consists of statements relating to time, in which the tenses are determined by the perspective in which the speaker at the present time regards them.

Be this as it may, the apparently obvious distinction between language and its subject simplifies their relationship in an unfortunate way. Both are always entangled with one another. Language is related to its subject in that it always in some degree contains the thing with which it is concerned. Of course the utterances of language can be understood as merely referring to things which are there before your eyes, so that they could really be replaced by pointing. But this is obviously a quite untypical extreme case of the utterances of language. The specific function of language – and so its necessity – becomes clear only when the subject with which it is concerned is not recognizable or present, or not immediately so, from the point of view of those who are speaking, and only becomes present through the utterances of language. Thus making present the past and the future and bringing to light what is hidden are the characteristic tasks of language. To describe the function of language as that of a sign is not sufficient to describe this relationship to its subject. Rather, language brings about an encounter with the subject itself. One can describe the direction of the movement which leads to this either by saying that language brings the hearer to the thing, or that it brings the thing to him.

But the reverse is also true. The subject does not just exist in isolation from language. Of course a distinction must be made here. Things and situations which are expressed in language can of course already be accessible in their own very different ways. But as soon as something which can be directly perceived by the senses is truly perceived – that is, when it is recognized and identified for what it is – then language comes into play even before the explicit act of speech takes place. The subject concerned is understood in connection with something else. It is distinguished from it and related to it. In short, the seeds of the whole process of categorizing it and forming judgments about it at various levels is already present (depending upon the point of view from which it is being regarded).

Consequently experience as such is always linguistic in nature from the first. For whether I experience something, and what I experience, does not depend solely upon the receptivity of the senses. It also depends upon the capability to perceive its meaning, and upon an ability, already available, to define something as something, to regard something from some point of view, to relate something to something else, to compare it with something else, to see it in a relationship of cause, result or purpose, etc. This can be clearly seen in individual cases in the way in which, in the situation of a particular experience, different people will perceive something quite different; that is, their experience is not the same. When witnesses are questioned afterwards this becomes startlingly obvious in the different statements they make. The idea that the apprehension of the subject, the perception itself, is as it were a naked fact, not clothed with language until later, is as false as the hope that one can penetrate to the pure truth by removing the outer veils of language.

Nevertheless, there are cogent reasons for the distinction between language and its subject. It is in the interest of the indivisible link between them to be aware of these reasons. The tendency of both elements to become mutually isolated and independent shows the necessity of emphasizing the distinction. It is required in order to avoid the danger of their alienation from one another, and in order to maintain the right relationship between them. Language can take on a life of its own, so that it no longer has its feet upon the solid ground of facts and loses its relationship to experience. Examples of this can be found in the various forms of literalism, of a credulous trust in words which does not pose the question of their verification. Sometimes particular statements are promulgated in an authoritarian fashion, and people accept them without testing them or thinking about them. Sometimes ill-considered assertions are made and brought into currency and roll on, as it were under their own momentum, in the same way as rumours. Another example again lies in the possibility of conducting a train of thought in terms of certain conceptions and ideas, arbitrarily relating them and drawing consequences from them, without ever exposing the whole tissue of ideas to verification by reality. The use of language, it must be affirmed, imposes not merely the condition that it should be correct in itself, in terms of language, but above all the condition that it be true. Consequently any statement of language requires verification, which can only be done by a critical confrontation between language and its subject, however such a confrontation may be defined in detail.

But the problem of things taking on a life of their own, in isolation from language, also arises in a similar way. They can become separated and isolated from the context of understanding that is displayed by language, or can be related to an artificially restricted context. It is also possible to abandon oneself unthinkingly to the immediate impression that they make and to become an uncritical victim to the factual claim they make, which seems obvious. Against this must be set the experience that reality is revealed by being understood and conveyed in language, that the senses are sharpened by an openness to meaning and relationships, and that direct experience takes on profundity and range, clarity and truth, only when it is brought out of the oppressive closeness of the immediate impression and set out in language. Not until this is done do we realize what has been impressed upon us. For that reason, given the differences between the two cases, one can also talk of the necessity of verification with regard to things – so that the criterion of the subject is found in language and that of language in its subject. Man's position is always within this circular process, in which his human contact with things is constituted by a contact with them through language, and his use of language is in contact with its subject.

e. The Possession of Language and the Authority to Use it

A final polarity which must be considered can be described as the distinction between the possession of language and the authority to use it. A person may be able to handle a language brilliantly, but this does not protect him from having nothing to say. Linguistic skill does not guarantee a convincing and authoritative use of language. This point of view can lead to a number of very different observations. We shall restrict ourselves to the question of the conditions under which the distinction becomes acute and perceptible. There is reason to suppose that this will lead us back to the very source of what takes place in language. We shall ignore for the moment the obvious objection that the whole problem can be solved by the distinction between language as mere outward form, and the content of what is uttered. We refer to what we have already said about the polarity between potentiality and act. And we may also expect that the discussion that follows will make clear how intimate a link there is between what a facile schematization would separate by the absolute use of the distinction between form and content. In fact it is only applicable in a relative sense.

We shall begin with the extreme experience that language sometimes completely fails us. Of course we are not concerned, or are only incidentally concerned, with the commonplace possibility that there ultimately has to be an end to talk, and the distinction becomes clear between the time to speak and the time to keep silent. The silence, of course, can be that of silent activity or perhaps even the silence which as such is both eloquent and active. If an undisciplined flow of speech comes to an end, for whatever reason, we breathe again. But the experiences which we have in mind now are in direct contrast to these. They take our breath away.

One of the most striking passages in the Book of Job, which is so rich in expressive images, is the account of what happens when the three friends come to Job.[48] They have heard of his misfortune, and their friendship requires them to seek their friend out in his misfortune. We can read between the lines that this was not easy for them. Who would not have shirked a duty of friendship of this kind? I am not happy to remember that as a young pastor, on my weekly visits to the hospital, where I was chaplain to one department, I sometimes turned past the hospital to the nearby woods, because it seemed too hard a task for me to find words in response to suffering. And we feel our own impotence in the face of a friend suffering perhaps even more strongly than with patients who are strangers to us. Job's friends, we read, made an appointment to go to him together. They obviously needed to lend each other courage, and arranged a meeting because one of them on his own might have found himself too weak. For it is clear from the start that they could do nothing to help; all they could do was to mourn over their friend, so stricken by fate, and comfort him. In such a situation words are all there is left to offer. That is, if they are still available, and one can bring oneself to utter them. The pain felt by someone who can only sit by and give comfort is a real participation in another's suffering, going far beyond what is usually understood by the feeling of compassion. It is a real sharing in the hopelessness of the situation.

It is understandable that Job's friends were at first able to do nothing but mourn: 'And when they saw him from afar, they did not recognize him; and they raised their voices and wept; and they rent their robes and sprinkled dust upon their heads toward heaven.' This was a wordless lamentation with tears and signs of distress. They could not reconcile what they saw with the picture of Job which they remembered. There was a cruel difference between the former Job and the Job they saw now. And where no connection is recognizable any longer, understanding fails. And where understanding fails, language is silent. All one can do is to express inarticulately, with the gestures usual on such occasions, that one is faced with something incomprehensible, which words can no longer describe. This was the only way in which the friends could enter into Job's new situation. And it meant a profound change in their own situation. Nor must this reaction on their part be dismissed merely as an oriental tendency to exaggeration. We may sometimes have wished ourselves to have been able to give such uninhibited expression to our suffering and compassion. What looks like greater control may well be the consequence of insensitivity.

But the story takes on even darker tones, which can scarcely be anything other than hyperbole: 'And they sat with him on the ground seven days and seven nights, and no one spoke a word to him, for they saw that his suffering was very great.' Imagine them sitting there side by side, without saying a single word, even for only an hour. One would begin to worry about how one's mind could stand the strain. Although words could have changed nothing, they might perhaps have made being together in this way somewhat less intolerable. Best of all perhaps, they might have been able to distract Job from his present misery. To speak about the past would of course hardly have been much use. That would only have been to rub salt into his wounds. To let the imagination play on the future would have been just as inappropriate. For the precondition of all imagination about the future is that there should clearly be some room for movement in it, at one's own disposal, to be given concrete form in one way or another. But for Job all this had been lost, together with what, when it is there, gives the future substance, but when it is absent makes it empty: his property, his children, his health. He was a man without hope, so deprived of hope in life and confidence in life that not even the recollection of the days when his life had been good, prosperous and happy could prevail against it. In retrospect, even they had lost their splendour. The past, like the future, had lost its meaning. As his death approached, he cursed the day of his birth.

There could only be silence, then, about his past and his future, since anything said about them would have been too loud, cruel and unequivocal, and would have brought them too close. And one might suppose that to speak of things of little importance would have been a relief. There may be cases in which it does no harm to practise a bit of trivial diversion therapy. It needs a little humour if it is to succeed. To judge by their later utterances, this was not the strong point of Job's friends. But that is not quite enough to explain why they did not seek to relieve him in this way. Of course in the face of the sufferings of Job, one could not just chatter about innocent everyday affairs. But could one not have used words of piety? This is what his friends had come for. They were devout men, and it is on these lines that one must imagine the comfort that they proposed to offer. But not even a single word of religious comfort crossed their lips, during seven days and seven nights, or at any rate for an unimaginably long time, during which they allowed the suffering of Job and nothing else, uninterruptedly and without opposition, to make its impression upon them, and be seen to take hold of them. This is an example of how human the Bible is. Job's friends were sensitive to the fact that it would have been impious to make pious remarks. You cannot bring the right thing to say ready-made to such a situation, and hand it over like a bunch of flowers as a sign of friendly sympathy. You must first let the floods of suffering flow over yourself, till you are at the point of succumbing to them, before you can dare to utter the words which can prevail in such circumstances, and which will bring true relief. Those who came to bring comfort had first to reconcile themselves to playing a comfort-less role, rather than simulating the comfort which would have left Job and themselves uncomforted. In such a case it is a poor comfort, but in reality the only comfort that is possible, to bear, sustain and share another's comfortlessness.

It was not one of the friends, but Job himself who broke the silence and expressed his suffering in such comfortless, if not godless, words that even the friends, one after the other, saw themselves as challenged to give an answer. And the answer they gave stuck closely to what Job had said and no longer to his suffering. Its purpose was no longer to comfort him, but to correct and instruct him. To give a comforting answer to

Job's words, they would probably have had to respond to them with another seven days and seven nights of silence.

The scene we have described is representative of the numerous ways in which, when faced with what is monstrous, we can be robbed of speech. That death imposes silence is true not merely in the physical sense that the loss of all bodily functions of course brings with it the loss of speech. It is also true of those whom death has spared, but who are so moved by it that, though they are called to say something, they are incapable of it, although they are still in full possession of the power of speech. That death is something natural and taken for granted does not cancel out its existential incomprehensibility. The main way, but not the only way, in which this is experienced is in the fact that the dead man is silent, that he can no longer be reached by words, and that this is not something fortuitous and transitory, but is final. If one tries to define, however, why the event of death has a destructive effect on language, one must take one's enquiry further, and point to the fact that death as such does not bestow anything to say at all. And you can only say anything about something, if it bestows of itself something to say.

That there is simply nothing to say about death, however, can easily be concealed by the fact that there exists, as it were on the margin of death, a multitude of experiences which press for utterance. The circumstances, causes and consequences of a death give material for discussion which can be inexhaustible. The painful wound of one who is deprived of part of his life can cause him to utter moving laments, which are inexhaustible in a different sense, not because they have so much to utter from numerous different points of view, but because all they can and must do is to go on monotonously repeating the same thing. Finally, the effort to resist the destructive effect of death usually releases a flow of words in the form of speeches about the achievements of the departed, general phrases of condolence, commonplace or devout reasons for taking comfort, and so forth. Of course there is a justifiable purpose in all this. But when we look at the heart of the matter we see that it is all a question of avoiding the fact that there is nothing to be said about death as such, that it does not allow us to say anything. For all we experience is the effects in life which accompany it; but we do not experience death itself. There is nothing for us to say about it, because it remains silent itself, and so does not itself become a phenomenon in any way. But this does not mean that it does not affect us, or does not force us to react to it and say something. Even avoidance is an answer to the challenge it makes which, inarticulate as it is, provokes articulation, at least in the form of a question. Death can neither be talked out nor hushed up. Words that are adequate to death and a protest against it which can carry weight must draw upon a different experience from that described. They must be based on an experience which does not repress the power of death to strike us dumb, and yet has the authority to overcome it.

We must make it quite clear that our argument is concerned not with the problem of death but with that of language. Death is taken, as it were, as a test case for the problem of language. I must also stress that I am not simply concentrating upon an isolated extreme case. Rather, it is a question of examining the vanishing point of all experiences, in which language is of no use to us, because the whole structure of understanding has collapsed and there is no possibility of breaching the gap through language.

There is also an experience of a somewhat different kind, in which we are forced to silence not by the irruption of the monstrous from outside, but by the loss of our own legitimization. There are situations in which I must keep silence, because I lack the right to open my mouth to speak. There are a number of stories in the gospels in which Jesus, in Luther's vivid translation, stops his opponents' mouths, by revealing that they lack any legitimate right to speak. The most impressive example of this is the situation in which, so it seems, Jesus is confronted by a crystal-clear and unequivocal case: an adulteress caught in the act, whom the law of Moses commanded to be stoned.[49] 'What do you say about her?' the scribes and Pharisees ask of Jesus, not because they have any doubt, but because they are so sure of their case. Jesus, it appears, has no choice but to submit to the authority of the law and therefore to lose his own authority, the authority of the gospel, or else, by resisting the authority of the law, to reveal the authority he had arrogated himself as one which publicly approves of adultery. With his very delayed and carefully thought-out answer: 'Let him who is without sin among you be the first to throw a stone at her', he reverses the question of legitimate authority in an astonishing way. Even a sacred text does not do away with the question of the right to apply it, to appeal to it on one's own account. Anyone who takes seriously the authority of the law should be the first to submit himself to it. Thus the judge is at once placed under judgment, the accuser is required to confess his own guilt and slinks away, because there is nothing more he can say. And the accused is set free.

It is no accident that this demonstration of the lack of any legitimate right to condemn, by asking whether the accuser submits to the authority to which he appeals, becomes evidence of the effective authority of Jesus. It displays this in two respects: as authority to unmask pretence and as authority to forgive. It is necessary to emphasize this, because it would be possible to make an illegitimate claim to outside authority here, in the same way as the scribes and Pharisees. For what grounds could one have to imitate Jesus in denying the legitimate right of a judge by asking whether he was without sin, as a condition of passing judgment? Would this not be the end of all human order? And what grounds could one have for using the fact that the accusers are also guilty to drop the accusation, and indeed to change it into a pardon? Here again we are not concerned with the specific problems with regard to the understanding of sin and forgiveness which are raised in this story in connection with an example of flagrant adultery. To go further into this would lead us to the distinction between the language of the law and the language of the gospel. But we are concerned at the moment only with pointing out the relevance of the question of legitimate authority for the problem of language as a whole.

Using words raises the question of the right to utter them. What permits someone to say something? What gives him the right and the freedom to do this? Let us look at this first from a negative point of view. Who are you to dare to say this? In some circumstances to ask this is to forbid someone to speak. He has no freedom to utter something. He is restricted and inhibited. There can be a wide range of possible causes for this. Apart from personal guilt, there can also be the fear of exposing oneself by what one says. For it is often impossible to separate the person who says something from what he says. And what is said is often given weight only by the fact that this particular person dares to say it in this situation. The possibility that someone may keep silence for fear of the consequences of what he says shows very clearly how language and its situation are intertwined. The circumstances which themselves urge one to say something can at the same time act as a barrier to speech. What is pressing to be spoken is held back and suppressed because the courage is lacking to utter it and to take responsibility for it. A particularly appropriate illustration can be found in examples of how in particular political situations the obvious remains unsaid. They make it clear how much power is attributed to language, to the extent that its free development is brought to a stop by constraints upon free speech. The public expression of opinion is intimidated, there is censorship of the press, public meetings are forbidden, and authors are prohibited from writing. In critical situations, of course, mere suggestion, a terror not physically exercised, but only spread by atmosphere, is often sufficient to impose silence. Thus example makes particularly clear the structure of the problem which we are approaching from various sides.

Of course one possesses the power of speech. And one knows *what* is to be said. But the ability to break the spell of silence is lacking. Here again, it would be too easy to separate the different aspects and exclude the courage to speak from the sphere of the problem of language. For the source of courage, and the cause of the lack of courage, must ultimately be sought where what is to be said turns into the authority actually to say it. The issue is obviously that a person is not sufficiently full of what is to be said, not completely convinced of what is seeking to be uttered, not unreservedly one with the word that is waiting to be spoken. The possible variations of such inhibitions upon language can be pursued as far as the individual psychological phenomenon of a speech impediment expressed in stuttering, an unconquerable fear of speaking in public, and so forth. Or the lack of courage to speak can be looked at from a different point of view again, such as that of repugnance, boredom, disgust with the surroundings, all of which can make it impossible to speak. A person may prefer to be silent, not because he lacks legitimate authority to speak but because it would lower his self-esteem to vouchsafe even a single word to his interlocutor, who is not a partner in any kind of dialogue. It would be casting pearls before swine. We shall give only two further examples from this vast complex of different ways in which people are prevented from speaking by the pressure of the situation of language.

The judgment whether it is justifiable and necessary to keep silence in a particular situation, or unjustifiable and blameworthy, is often difficult to make. Like all genuine decisions, it involves a personal risk. The predominant impression seems to be that the opportunities which make it a duty to speak are largely missed. But one must also remember that one sometimes has to take one's time and wait patiently until the moment to speak has come. Of course there is a danger that waiting for the right moment may become a facile excuse, so that the opportunity is not taken. How easy it is to speak too late, or even to realize that one should have unquestionably have said something or other, but now it would no longer be any use. But this observation does not mean that we should not take seriously the argument that we may be legitimately prevented from speaking because the time is not right. Thus a poet or philosopher may have to refrain from public utterance for years in order to allow a statement to mature in silence. Perhaps only in this way can we avoid its being lost at once in the general devaluation of language, or even accelerating that process. The choice of the right moment may instead let it play its part in restoring the value of language and authoritatively sweeping away the litter of worthless talk.

It is rare, of course, that the question whether the right moment has come imposes a really important choice between keeping silence and speaking out. One criterion might be that the choice cannot be made either way without pain. It must be difficult to keep silence. And one must be aware of the immense consequences which can ensue if one breaks silence. A striking historical example of such an awareness of the situation in the use of language is the letter of dedication with which Luther heads his 'Address to the Christian Nobility'. Referring to Ecclesiastes 3 :7, 'There is . . . a time to keep silence, and a time to speak', he begins with the affirmation: 'The time to keep silence is past and the time to speak has come.'[50] It is not easy to reproduce the emotional force of this statement with as much justification.

The pattern the problem displays is different again, when one considers the influence exercised on one's right, one's freedom to speak, by the interlocutor to whom and before whom one is speaking. Here again one comes upon a very complex situation. We have all encountered people in whose presence our words stick in our throats. Intentionally or not, justifiably or not, they spread an atmosphere of oppression, and with crushing violence destroy the freedom to speak. They do not radiate the confidence that invites us to confide in them. Every statement which goes beyond purely objective information and touches on the personal – even if this only happens through the context in which a fact is being communicated – is an act which invokes confidence, for through it one gives oneself to another person. On the other hand, I would hope that everyone has already experienced how an encounter with a person can have something totally liberating about it. It lightens the heart, loosens the tongue and gives freedom to say everything. But of course here again a distinction must be made. Leave to speak cannot be made generally dependent upon one's interlocutor, in the sense that he alone may give it. A watch has to be kept for what, in the face of every barrier of mistrust and hostility, may give the freedom to speak. Of course it is freedom only if it is not a question of force being met by force, and a rough word being answered merely by another insult. Its place must be taken by an independence and ascendancy which enables the speaker to utter words that create freedom, overcome mistrust and clear away the atmosphere of terror and fear. That is, I give the other person the freedom which he appears to deny to me and to threaten to take from me. On the other hand, the invitation to speak must not have the character of a compulsion, making it difficult to keep something to oneself. It would be worth looking for the source of the discipline of language which, in the face of the strongest urge and need to convey information, may sometimes require one to withhold it, and will give the strength to keep silent.

Within the field of the failures of language which bring to

light the gap between the possession of language and the authority to use it, we must therefore look at a further complex of phenomena. I am thinking of the fact, all too familiar, that a great expenditure of words can often result in little or nothing being said. Discourse turns into chatter. Language becomes mere form without content. When language is drained of meaning in this way, it is probably a sign that the speaker himself is as it were drained of meaning. The most trivial example of this is when someone runs out of material and yet still goes on talking, producing a kind of cardboard mock-up of language by means of repetitions and meaningless padding. Of course the flow of speech then dries up very promptly, confirming the simple truth that what fills the heart corresponds with what the mouth utters. And an empty heart also corresponds to a barren use of language, though that can of course be camouflaged by a torrent of words and must never be confused with the economical use of words.

If one wishes to consider the whole range of what can be uttered, one ought not of course to limit oneself to what urgently wells up from the heart. Every aspect of human learning is included here, beginning with factual knowledge, through a constant openness to new perceptions, and the power of judgment, to the wisdom which apprehends profound underlying connections and surveys the whole sphere in which language is at work. From each of these points of view it can be clearly seen that language lives by what a person has to say, and dies when a person has nothing more to say. If I am to impart knowledge, a certain degree of knowledge on my own part is needed. The ability to see decides whether I am able to convey my impressions and draw attention to phenomena. My power of judgment decides whether or not I can bring order and coherence, critical discrimination and judicious evaluation to the confusion of facts and opinions. And it is the task of wisdom to judge what is of first importance amongst the various competing utterances of language, and what is the right thing to say at a particular time. Wisdom too gives the ability to distinguish, with a reliable sense of tact, the time to speak and the time to keep silent. If these sources dry up, so does the flow of language, not merely in the quantitative sense, but above all with regard to its quality. The more barren and meagre the content of language, the more the formal richness of language declines, its sensibility, its subtlety, its autonomy and conscientiousness, its power and tenderness.

This draws our attention to the following consideration. The life of language is a unity in spite of the many different sources from which spoken language is nourished. I have summed them up as knowledge, a constant openness to new perceptions, the power of judgment, and wisdom. But the different aspects of what takes place in language can of course be developed to a very different degree in the same person. Thus, for example, one person may have a brilliant command of a particular technical language, while in the language of personal intercourse he moves at an extremely modest level, as can be seen, say, from his conversation or in the style of his letters. This is no objection to the argument that the life of language is a unity. But it does make us aware that interruptions in the rate of growth can occur in this single life of language, leading to hypertrophy on one side and atrophy on the other. This is why situations of this kind are felt to be signs of something wrong. For we cannot ignore the relationships between different parts of the whole spectrum of language, such as come to light in their actual effects on one another. The following examples will make clear what we mean. For a specialist activity which is meant to be not merely reproductive but truly creative, a breadth of vision and openness to other realms of speech is an indispensable condition. Or again, if communication, even on technical and specialist matters, is to be a living thing, qualities are required other than those peculiar to the specialism, such as a willingness to engage in dialogue and a readiness to agree. On the basis of this intimate link between life and language, centred as it is upon the person of the speaker, one can assert that, notwithstanding the many sources of the utterances of language, the source of language is ultimately the heart.

The link between the life of the heart and the life of language, however, is no doubt of greater complexity than can be described from the purely quantitative aspect of fullness or emptiness. Crises in language are by no means always due to the withering away of the inner life, to the drying up of the sources of what we have to say. There are other causes of breakdown, related to the process of the formation of language itself, which have to be taken into account. Of course we must warn against simplifying the matter in the other direction. The difficulties do not lie solely in the task of finding the right expression for what one would like to say. Often, in trying to make a precise statement, we have to search for a particular word or a certain turn of phrase. Often we find the possibilities of expression which they offer to be inadequate, reject them, and do not rest content until we find the phrase that hits the mark. As we see from this, our wrestling with the form of language brings us face to face with the discrepancies between what we really mean to say and the way in which we provisionally attempt to say it, until finally we breach this gap as best we can. Often it is simply a matter of recollecting an expression which has slipped our memory, but which we know is still in the back of our mind. We must not present a one-sided view by forcibly limiting the great variety of such causes of difficulty with language. But looking at the matter as a whole we can say that difficulties of language always reflect difficulties of content. Even when it is only a matter of my not being able to use an expression which, as we say, is on the tip of my tongue, I have not yet clearly thought out the state of affairs I need it to formulate. Thus this difficulty is not merely one of stating clearly to others, and imparting to others, something which I have already clearly comprehended for myself. Formulation in language is not merely a secondary occasion – as it were the packaging or the vehicle – of passing on what lies there ready, independently of this process. Rather, the process of thought is so much a process of language that it does not attain its goal until it has reached the point of definition in language. For this reason, the problems which sometimes arise in giving verbal form to thought are not something additional to the understanding of the substance of the matter. They always form part of the true understanding of the matter, even though their degree of relevance varies considerably.

Wrestling for verbal expression is always, therefore, a wrestling to understand the substance of the matter which it is intended to utter. We cannot dismiss as mere aesthetic formalism the sensibility which will not rest content with the first suitable expression that comes to hand, with a familiar turn of phrase, but hunts fastidiously and with a delicate precision for the most appropriate form of language. This is part of a conscientious concern for a clear understanding of the matter. Quite often the right word is not found, because the struggle for a new and genuine understanding of a matter – or in broader terms, for a new and genuine understanding of reality altogether – is under way, but has not yet been brought to a clear conclusion. This is as it were the travail caused by a life which is there already but has not yet fully come into the world. But through these very pains it is seeking to come into the world. Thus the cause of a failure of language can be traced back not to a lack of content in the statement, but to a superabundance of material, not yet clarified, but struggling violently for articulation, and consequently choked in the process of coming to utterance. Anyone affected by a very powerful experience, and seeking in his excitement to describe it, can scarcely utter a word, because the way he puts it cannot keep pace with the rush with which his experience bursts out of him. And how often stuttering and babbling can be signs not of poverty of spirit, but of an abundance, albeit still chaotic, of enthusiastic emotion.

The tension between what is newly pressing to be uttered, and the still deficient language in which it is expressed, is due to the fact that in this case conventional language is felt to be inadequate. It is familiar, all too familiar. One actually has to guard against simply allowing oneself to be carried along without thinking by its current. Or, to use another metaphor, traditional language is handled in so well-practised and routine a fashion that it has become worn smooth and so has lost its grip. It is no longer capable of taking a fresh hold on reality and of reaching deep into it. When we take this issue further, we at once find ourselves in the midst of a tangled problem. The inadequacy may simply lie in the fact that ordinary language offers too little resistance in use, and creates too few tensions to require reflection. As a form of language which has already reached maturity, it requires no effort of us, but it also deprives us of the stimulation and profit of struggling to find words for something. Here begins the dialectic between the letter and the spirit, which Luther was very well aware of when he emphasized that it is a continuous process.[51] Something which now occurs to me and takes on verbal form, that is, which becomes fixed in letters, is still spirit to me while it is happening. And it is spirit exercising its specific power to take on concrete form and achieve definition. But what today is spirit to me in this way may well already have become the mere letter to me tomorrow, a ready-made legacy of language, handed down as a fixed law, which can only become spirit for me again if I go back to the origins of what happened when it was first uttered as language, taking it up and making it my own again. This process explains the frictions which occur in the course of the transition in history from one generation to another and from one mode of thought to another. Thus, for example, the achievements of the pioneers of dialectical theology, for which they had to fight against powerful resistance in an intensive process of understanding, were handed down to the generation that followed without a struggle. And so they underwent a change by the very fact that they were now principles taken for granted. To establish them no longer required personal struggle and suffering, so that the background against which they were experienced was no longer present. On the other hand the new basis itself provoked the attempt to go beyond it, to look for what agreed with it or contradicted it, and in both cases to establish something on the basis of one's own experience and knowledge.

What takes place here cannot adequately be understood as a mere change of vocabulary. Of course within certain limits this can also be shown to be necessary. Through intensive use certain words sooner or later become worn out. They undergo a process of inflation and lose their value. They are made to carry more and more meaning, lose definition, and finally come to mean everything and nothing. Then the moment comes when they are set aside altogether, and as it were are given leave of absence in order to recover – unless they are dismissed altogether as of no further use at all. But such a change of vocabulary only very rarely leads to the introduction of synonyms which are not worn out, but which merely say the same thing in a more lively and more accurate way. Other words bring other nuances with them, they imply different questions and change the pattern of the argument. Seen solely from the point of view of vocabulary, the change from one period to another, from one generation to another, and even from one fashion to another, can often be seen to consist only in the dominance of new key words, the rise of new party jargons and the conversion of the magic of words, which is deeply rooted in the use of language, to the worship of more effective idols. But something more profound takes place in the necessary and continuous endeavour to express ideas in language. This may be conducted in quiet and unspectacular processes, whenever there is a vigilant exercise of responsibility for contemporary language. From time to time, however, it may lead to breakthroughs and transformations on a large scale. But it goes deeper than the mere separation from one another of favourite themes and the swing of the pendulum of prevailing judgments and polemic emphases back and forward between the conservative and revolutionary reactions. This is the reason it is worth continuing to apply oneself to the great problems and principal tasks of mankind, on which work must go on all the time. Of course here and there new aspects and dimensions can be discovered. But for all our fascination with what is new, we must not avoid our responsibility for the continuity of language. And the endeavour to give new utterance to an idea is carried out with the necessary care only if there is at the same time a concern for the continuity of language in the new form of expression, a concern which, as a critical – and also self-critical – dialogue with the legacy of language, helps to bring about the improvement in language which is being sought.

Thus the aim of the struggle for a new expression in language is for a genuine and honest language in which the present experience of reality can be made accessible and can be mastered. One might also say that it is a matter of an authority to use language which is not directly present in a language which has become too familiar and which has become overloaded with other experiences. This creative process in language can take place at very different levels. The term 'creative' can be applied in the first place to the bringing into being of mechanisms and forms of language which assist a considerable number of people over a long period in their use of language, providing them with a kind of set framework of language. But I believe that the point of view of creativity in language draws attention to something which in a fundamental sense is expected of everyone in his use of language. We are inevitably exposed to the fact that ordinary language does not coincide directly with experience, and that there is therefore a constant possibility of a discrepancy between language and reality. Thus when we use the language handed down to us, we have to take account of whether it is adequate to our experience, or ask what experience we have to open ourselves to, in order to come to terms honestly with this received language. Moreover, in dealing with reality, we have to consider whether language may be being misused to obscure reality or whether it is helping to bring it to light and open it up to us, thus bringing it to utterance in an undistorted form. Even in the simplest responsible use of language there is an element of creativity. This takes the form of a flexibility with regard to language, a ready acceptance of the possibility of innovation, of familiar language perhaps becoming outdated and powerless, of a need to test received language and of the growth from experience of language which is genuine and honest. Of course taking this creative factor seriously does not absolve us from the constant realization of how much language fails us. We often lack the language to sum up clearly and to cope with the reality with which we are faced. And our own experience is quite often insufficient to back the language we rely on. If we are to be open to the creative factor in language we must stand firm in face of the pain of the alienation between language and reality. This is necessary whenever we come across in our own language what might be called unintegrated alien elements, something which eludes our understanding, or when we encounter in our own experience of reality the alienating element which has not been digested in terms of language and is difficult to cope with, something which cannot even be clearly articulated as a question and proves refractory to our understanding.

In this last group of phenomena we considered the polarity between the possession of language and the authority to use language largely in relationship to the difficulties which occur in the attempt to comprehend in language *what* has to be said. Let us now go on to consider it from the point of view of the persons concerned, the fact that language can fail in its function as an instrument of mutual assent. We have of course already hinted at this from time to time. For in reflecting on language it is difficult to ignore the fact that it is concerned with communication. It was in fact for this reason that we introduced this whole complex of problems with an example of how the irruption of something monstrous into human life does not merely deprive the individual of speech; rather, being deprived of speech when with other human beings is experienced as a condemnation to silence.

Let me recall once again the image of the four men sitting together, Job and his friends. They have a fellow-feeling towards each other. Everything as it were cries out for communication. And yet there are walls which separate them; each is shut off in his own cell, and it is not possible for them to communicate with each other, even though they are most intensely aware of the presence of the others and therefore of the breakdown of communications. One might recognize in this picture modern experiences in which silence, as the agony of an insurmountable loneliness in the midst of one's fellows, becomes an overwhelming fate. This is not the silence which, when one is in familiar company, can actually be the fruit of communication brought to fulfilment, and in its turn gives rise to new spoken communication. One might say of this latter kind of silence, that it is a test of true fellowship for people to be able not merely to talk to one another but also to keep silence with one another, and that mutual understanding and assent is actually furthered in silence. In this form silence becomes a necessary element in the life of language. But the extreme experience of silence as a total loss of communication goes far beyond what happened in Job's house. Here the silence was still a testimony of friendship, though of course of a friendship which could offer no help. It was still the expression of a helplessness which could look forward to something better. It was not silence in the definitive sense, without any hope of communication. In a sense this solidarity in helplessness and lack of comfort is a most moving expression of a continuing faith in the possibility of communication. This silence, lasting seven days and seven nights, was not an apathetic fading away into a final loss of language. Rather, it was a tense, urgent expectation of the reception of words capable of breaking the silence. And thus in spite of all it was a hopeful, and not a despairing silence. Yet we are also aware of the fearful possibility of hopeless silence, this paradoxical medium in which human beings can live their lives in company and yet in isolation. Any words uttered in this situation have no more than the technical function of traffic signals, and human beings themselves are no longer touched by them.

Let us now go on from this extreme aspect to look for a further variety in the possibilities of a breakdown of mutual assent. We do so once again only to indicate how tangled the undergrowth of problems is. We must begin from the fact that the event of language itself brings with it difficulties of understanding and the achievement of assent. Fortunately the exchange which takes place in language is usually carried out without problems. There is usually no reason to be aware of how complicated a process is taking place. For language in essence is not that which creates difficulties of understanding, as one might suppose from the impression given by hermeneutic and interpretative activities and concerns which have been misunderstood or carried out in a misleading fashion. Rather, language is that which reveals and conveys understanding. The basic phenomenon is not the understanding *of* language, but understanding *by means* of language. Yet it cannot be said that the mere occurrence of difficulties of understanding and assent in itself represents a breakdown of the function of language. Indeed, language displays its hermeneutic power in the fact that it does not capitulate in the face of such difficulties, but rather finds in them the tasks by which it grows and develops until it can overcome the resistances and, in so doing, sometimes work miracles. We are thinking here not merely of the removal of the difficulties of understanding produced by obscure and inadequate verbal utterances, which can of course be removed by purely verbal means. Language displays its power in the first instance by bringing light and clarity into the confusion and oppressive darkness of our experience of the world and by establishing a fellowship between men. This it does by providing the basis of the teaching and learning which makes man what he is, so opening to him infinite possibilities of communication and at the same time making him capable of repairing breakdowns in communication. Perhaps the most profound mystery of language is that through it we can reach the heart of another, even though we have no control over how it is received by the person to whom we are speaking; and that language that goes to the heart can even change the heart. Let us look at two examples of this coexistence of the extreme power of language and our lack of control over it as we use it. The examples we choose cast a particularly clear light on the problem of the breakdown of communication.

Somewhat pretentiously, one might say that the hermeneutic task which enjoins us to be concerned for understanding, wherever understanding is in question, and for mutual assent, at the very point where it is scarcely to be hoped for, forms an important part of what has recently been proclaimed a new branch of research, that is, research into the means of bringing about peace. The fundamental difficulty in the problem of achieving peace, however, consists of finding out how to establish the basic condition which makes any mutual assent possible – that is, a genuine willingness to achieve mutual assent. How can the confidence be aroused which does not look at what one's interlocutor says with a basic suspicion, seeing it against a background of concealed thoughts and underhand intentions, and so robbing it of its validity from the very first? And how instead can one find the courage to take the other at his word, and sometimes even achieve such authority in one's words as to reach him and create confidence in him? Think for a moment of the barriers to be overcome in this respect even in the relationship between individual persons, or within such a small social unit as a university. One must surely confess that in view of the multiplicity and confusion of language throughout the world, the scale of the problems becomes immense. The hermeneutic task would be purely academic if one did not take into account, in considering it, this aspect of the effort to achieve mutual assent on a world-wide scale, and the question of the sources of mutual confidence throughout the world.

The other example concerns the often discussed issue of the way language becomes worn out and superficial, until it is no more than an instrument of information, and the aspect of what is beyond our control when language is in use is consciously excluded. Here language is denied its essential and most profound task, that of accepting responsibility for the mystery of reality, in order to preserve it as a mystery.

The sinister thing, however, about the reduction of language to a technical instrument lies not simply in the fact that it results in the neglect of whole dimensions of life, which quite often then take their revenge and make themselves felt in unpleasant ways. What is threatening and disturbing above all is that language can become an instrument through which the human heart itself can be manipulated. Think, for example, of the technique of commercial advertising and of propaganda in politics or on behalf of particular world views (including misdirected religious propaganda). Language, the essentially human in mankind, can be abused in order to dehumanize man. The task of a theory of language in the most ambitious sense therefore consists of a defence of the humanity of language, for the sake of the language of humanity.

CHAPTER III

Scepticism about a Mere Theory of Language

I. FORMS OF A THEORY OF LANGUAGE HANDED DOWN FROM ANTIQUITY

The concept of a theory of language, what it can achieve, and what can be expected of it, obviously needs to be clarified. Let us first note the forms the theory of language has taken from early times and how, even from the point of view of terminology, they have differed. Of course it is not sufficient merely to list the terms used in each case. For – as is inevitable in the sphere of the problem of language – when each term is considered more closely, the appearance of a clearly delineated phenomenon dissolves into a constant motion. When the problems are fluid in this sense, it becomes extraordinarily difficult to define them. Consequently we shall now outline a number of the forms taken by the theory of language, but we shall be unable to go into each one in depth. We must be content to understand the tasks which they formulate, and to become aware of a number of problems related to them in order to take account of them later, as far as we need to and are able. But above all we shall try to define more accurately and clarify what it means to speak of a theory of language in general and of a theological theory of language in particular.

The general education inherited from antiquity and given a formal scholastic structure when it was adopted by the Middle Ages is known as the *artes liberales*. Its basis lies in the three branches of knowledge – known as the *trivium* – which are concerned with language or words: grammar, rhetoric and dialectic. The *quadrivium* which followed it consists of the branches of knowledge which are concerned with numbers: arithmetic, geometry, music and astronomy. Whatever the particular ideal of education and its realization in detail, any coherent elementary instruction will always make its first task that of improving the knowledge and use of language. Language is not one art amongst many, all of which it is useful in life to have learnt and to be able to exercise. Rather, it is the medium in and through which all other teaching and learning takes place; as it were, the element in which they live. Even the teaching of technical crafts cannot be carried out without language. Of course one can pass on certain techniques and skills simply by showing them to people, and they can pick them up by imitation. But how limited man's ability to teach and learn is in this respect, until language has been developed, can be seen from the difficulty that is found in teaching children whose language development is retarded to carry out meaningful activity on the most modest level. For even the simplest manual activity is related to an aim and forms part of a plan, and therefore forms part of a context of understanding which assumes language and makes tacit use of it, even if no words are used in inculcating it. The famous 'Aha!' effect illustrates this. It is the spontaneous expression of the fact that something has dawned upon me, that I have understood something.

That learning and teaching are a process carried out by language is most clearly seen in the necessary and inextricable interpenetration of theory and practice. But for this reason, in order to make a proper distinction between them, so that they aid each other and do not introduce confusion into each other, it is essential that when anything is being taught theory and practice should to some extent be kept apart. What in essence can only be carried out by language (that is, theory) must to some extent maintain its independence with regard to that which, though it is not of its nature completely inexpressible in language, is largely not carried out by means of language (that is, practice). Of course it must be emphasized that there are kinds of practice which are exercised by the direct use of language. Teaching and learning themselves are a particular kind of practice.

a. Grammar

Grammar undoubtedly has the nature of an elementary theory of language. Yet from the first this statement must be qualified and corrected. It sounds commonplace to point out that one does not learn a language by grammar, but this draws our attention to something important. Within the whole phenomenon of teaching and learning language, instruction in grammar is a quite distinct and secondary aspect. No one learns to speak by acquiring rules of grammar. Nor does sensible instruction in learning a foreign language proceed in this way. One learns language by learning communication through language. And a certain familiarity with language is a condition of instruction in grammar. In fact the teaching of the elements of reading and writing is a first stage and a necessary precondition of instruction in grammar. As the word 'grammar' ('the study of letters') betrays, an awareness of grammar can only be developed on the basis of a language which has been put into letters, that is, into written language. This is a sign of something important which should be recorded in passing.

The importance of writing for language goes much further than the mere provision of a means for preserving language. That man is capable of giving endurance to language outside the transitory act of speech is a revolutionary factor in regard to the phenomenon of language, going far beyond mere preservation. It opens up completely new dimensions to language. In the first place, it is only this which makes language an object of study, in the sense that explicit reflection can begin upon its structure and rules. For the spoken articulation of a language becomes something which can be realized and represented as an object only when it is put into written form. The more abstract and economical the forms which represent this articulation – as attained by the transition from ideograms to an alphabet – the more precise must be the analysis of the process of articulation. The breaking down of language into a small number of letters, which allow an infinite number of combinations, is in itself an act of reflective analysis on a high level, breaking through superficial appearances and apprehending in abstract form what is not directly perceptible. Accordingly, it also leads to the study of the rules which are unconsciously applied in language. Thus the development of grammar assumes the existence of a high degree of reflection upon language, something which is not required in the mere use of language. Thus any theory of language is always a demanding process of reflection, requiring one to stand back from language as it is directly spoken. Thus a theory of language is something quite different from the direct act of communication involved in teaching language. Rather, it always implies an explicit and methodical objectivization of the living process of language.

This raises the following question, which forms a preliminary to what we shall go on to consider. How far is a theory of language an appropriate means of dealing with the difficulties which arise in our use of language? Clearly the need for a theory of language arises in the end from breakdowns of language. But can language be put to rights by a theory *about* language? The implications of our heading 'Scepticism about a Mere Theory of Language' have their roots in the impression that there can be difficulties with language which cannot be overcome by a theory of language. And these may well be the problems which create the worst difficulties with regard to language. This reason at least explains, perhaps somewhat prematurely, why a theological theory of language may encounter scepticism. The grave problems of theology seem in fact to be of such a nature that a theory of language has very little to contribute to them. Such a theory clearly assumes the particular language in question and relates to it. Thus in the case of theology such a theory would have its place *within* theology and – at least so it appears – could not involve itself with the problems which might call into question the language of theology and therefore the subject of theology as a whole. And there seems to be even less promise in the suggestion of breathing new life into a language by a theory of language.

So what is the function of a purely grammatical theory of language? It makes us aware of the rules which provide the structure of language: how individual words have to be declined and conjugated and how they are put together in sentences. In appropriate cases other branches of linguistic science such as historical philology, etymology, semantics and morphology can come into play. But we can ignore this for the moment. The setting up and systematizing of the rules of the language, together with the exceptions to them, which can also be more or less firmly established and cannot be dealt with arbitrarily, as well as the scope for free choice between equally balanced possibilities in accidence and syntax, are meant to be an aid to the correct use of the language. This does not mean that a correct use of the language is not possible without grammatical knowledge. The opposite is very much the case, as can be seen from the fact that all grammar ever does is to derive its rules from the language as it is actually spoken; it cannot prescribe arbitrary rules for it. Besides, while grammar assists in bringing about a *correct* use of language, it cannot ensure that a person speaks a language really *well*. This requires a training in the language which above all gives a sound linguistic feeling for the personal handling of the language that cannot be summed up in rules and produced with the aid of rules. However incapable grammar may be of achieving this, its necessity in avoiding errors of language is obvious. In learning a foreign language it is consequently much more necessary to know the grammar than in the case of one's own language: for one never knows a foreign language so well. For this reason, in fact, the grammar of foreign languages is usually much more consciously understood than the rules of one's own language, which one takes for granted, but of which one is unaware. Nevertheless, a concern with the grammar of one's own language is valuable in using it, because it leads to a high degree of awareness of language. And in addition to its aid in the correct use of language and this awareness of language, the grammatical theory of language is also of aid in understanding. The knowledge of grammatical rules makes possible the analysis of complicated sentences, and provides criteria for dealing with difficulties of translation. Finally, grammar leads to the understanding of the logic of language. Its particular use, by contrast with purely formal logic, is that it gives an insight into the characteristic structures of thought and understanding of reality in a given language, as for example in the understanding of time which is found in it.

Let us briefly mention two statements which take a critical view of the usual understanding of a grammatical theory of language. The way in which language is interpreted on the basis of its grammatical rules and the schematic pattern into which they force the life of the language can in some circumstances restrict and be a burden to thought. One may ask whether the categories of classical grammar, and in particular the dominance of grammatical thought about language, may not also have produced very unfortunate historical effects. Eugen Rosenstock-Huessy, in his works on the philosophy of language, has vehemently proclaimed the idea of a 'grammar as it really is' in opposition to the prevailing grammar. He compares its importance to the Copernican revolution.[52] Somewhat differently, Luther argued against the way in which scholastic grammar was taken for granted and became the dominant logical standard, even for theology, with the axiom: 'The Holy Spirit has his own grammar.'[53] Or again, 'If one wishes to speak of God, the whole of grammar must adopt new words. For even the series of numbers, "one, two, three", cannot be applied here. It holds for creatures, but here there is no order in number, space and time. Consequently we have to do something quite different here and lay down a different mode of expression from the natural one.'[54] This sounds very wrong, as though theological language were excused from the general logic and standards of language. Statements of this kind make people suspicious of every attempt at a specifically theological theory of language, a *philologia sacra*. But of course anyone who is at all familiar with Luther's attitude to language will not suspect him of trying to set himself free arbitrarily from grammatical precision. For it was he who laid down as a basic principle of theological hermeneutics: 'First we have to look at grammar, for it is in fact of theological significance.'[55] And whatever criticism may be made of the way he speaks of a new grammar of the Holy Spirit, at least it puts in words the question whether the usual grammar can claim to be regarded as the norm for the intrinsic logic of the most varied aspects of reality. Or is there not a necessity to supplement the limited function of a grammatical theory of language by theories of language of a different kind?

b. Rhetoric

It was, of course, from a different point of view that in antiquity rhetoric was introduced as yet another kind of theory of language in addition to grammar. The distinction could be made in this way: while grammar was the *scientia recte loquendi*, the nature of rhetoric could be defined as *ars bene dicendi*. Of course the second assumed and included the first. No one can make a good use of language if he does not understand how to use it correctly. Of course this is only true with qualifications. It may well be that a poetic use of language breaks the bonds of grammar and is permitted a licence which goes beyond the limits of what is correct. One of the symptoms of the crisis of language at the present day is the fact that the language of poetry sometimes comes into conflict with grammar. This is not because errors of grammar are made from ignorance. Rather, there is an attempt to wrest from language a power of statement which cannot be achieved without occasionally breaking the usual rules, without a startling abandonment of the customary usage of language, without a protest against the pedantry of a ready-made logic or aesthetic of language, and without creative freedom (although it is often difficult to tell the difference between the mere show of purely destructive liberty and the presence of a genuine creative freedom). Thus, for example, if one approaches a poem by Paul Celan with the traditional standards of correct grammar and stylistic purity, it is not merely the relationship between *recte loqui* and *bene dicere*, but the understanding of *recte* and *bene* themselves which is once again called into question and made to appear fluid. But to demonstrate that the classical forms of grammar and rhetoric (and the theory of poetry associated with them) can be called into question in this way does not mean that they are simply made invalid. An arbitrary abandonment of grammatical rules would ultimately mean that the meaningful effects produced by certain transgressions of the limits would be absent. And even an extremely personal use of language, which resists standards in order to produce certain effects, assumes these standards. Not only does it assume them for the sake of contrast, but also because the breaking point of them depends upon the normal use of them.

It is no accident that the distinction between grammar and rhetoric has confronted us with the experience that the forms of a theory of language which come from antiquity, and which have determined the Western tradition of education, are not of course simply in abeyance, but are clearly inadequate to do justice to the problem of language with which we are faced at the present day. It is not that the use of language is undergoing a development which will not tolerate any kind of theory of language. On the contrary, one gets the impression that the symptoms of crisis to which I have referred make a theory of language, albeit of a different kind from the traditional forms, all the more urgent. And it may well be that the symptoms of crisis, in so far as they have a formative effect upon language, themselves provide certain starting points for a new theory of language. A conscious struggle with language always brings with it a reflection upon language. It is never more necessary to pay attention to the meaning of *recte* and *bene* with regard to the use of language than when their meaning has been profoundly questioned. The similar phenomena in the plastic arts or in music, where the traditional rules of artistic technique and aesthetics are similarly being denied and have to be transcended, are accompanied by the same tendency to conscious reflection with regard to the nature of the art as such.

Thus ancient rhetoric was directed towards the task of *bene dicere*. One must not hamper one's understanding of it by supposing that it was concerned only with the doubtful luxury of decorative and ornamental language. It was not seeking merely a refined way of adding a lustre to what one had to say by the way in which one said it, instead of depending simply upon the intrinsic impression made by what one said. Nor was it concerned, as is sometimes supposed, with the questionable art of concealing with the aid of intoxicating eloquence the fact that one fundamentally had nothing to say, by lulling to sleep, instead of arousing, the power of judgment by the methods of the demagogue, by standing truth on its head through the tricks of the advocate and by finding a way to justify anything. The Sophists were an early example of such a degradation of rhetoric. This largely determined the later understanding of it and gave the pejorative sense to the term 'rhetorical'. It should not prevent us from looking further at the genuine intentions of rhetoric.

Bene did not originally refer to the form of language at all. That is, to speak *bene* in addition to *recte* did not mean that one was at once suspected of falsification. That is, the term meant something more than merely a euphemistic expression for a wrong use of language. The expression *bene dicere alicui* means 'to speak good of someone'. This refers not primarily to the form of language, but to its content, and has in mind the effect the statement is intended to make. The aesthetic element in no sense exists in its own right, but is subordinated to moral purposes. One may recall Luther's use of the term 'to speak well of someone' in his interpretation of the commandment 'You shall not bear false witness against your neighbour'. He turns it into a positive command: We 'ought to forgive him and speak well of him and make the best of everything'.[56] Anyone who speaks good of someone is not of course required to say what is not true. On the contrary, he must maintain truth against untruth, and must do so as effectively as he possibly can. This is only right in view of the importance of what words can do in this case, and what they ought to achieve. For it is a matter of the reputation, the good name and the honour of a fellow human being; but when they are threatened it is not merely a question of his reputation, good name and honour, but of fundamental questions of his existential life. The expression *benedicere*, fused into a single word, comes in religious language to mean 'praise', 'bless'. (This word has been borrowed into German as the verb *benedeien*, with the same meaning.) It may seem strained to refer to this association of ideas in considering rhetoric as the *ars bene dicendi*. But it is not as far-fetched as it seems. It is wholly appropriate to the range of vision which rhetoric opens up for the problem of language that it can look as far as the ultimate possibilities of what language can effect.

By contrast to grammar as a theory of language, the novel and characteristic feature of the theory of language presented by rhetoric is that it reflects upon the use of language in the concrete sense. That is, it is concerned with how language is to be used in real life, what the requirements are on which its use is based, what dangers threaten it, in which situations its meaning is most intense, to which sociological conditions it is subject, and many other considerations of the same kind. It is the proper task of grammar, but also its ultimate limitation, that it looks at language as it were in suspense, in isolation from its concrete use, in order to dissect it anatomically and undertake laboratory experiments upon it. Thus it is characteristic that even the sentences which grammar uses for examples are often artificial compositions. They are really examples of how one does not usually speak. Rhetoric, on the other hand, pays attention to the *process* of language. It regards as fundamental the fact that language takes concrete form as speech. And in this process there are always at least two partners, the speaker and the person addressed. The problem then arises of how this process achieves what it is intended to achieve. Since it is something taking place between human beings, the ethical aspect becomes of importance.

The theoreticians of rhetoric discussed the question of the category of art or science to which it should be allocated. In the usual subdivision into theoretical, practical and poetic arts, rhetoric was usually characterized as a practical art, although the theoretical and poetic points of view of course made their contribution to it, and in some cases could even be more strongly emphasized. Thus rhetoric is concerned with the way in which practical use is made of language. And this practical use is more than a formal and neutral technique, for it concerns the way in which we cope with life itself. This brings us to an important focus of the problem of language as a whole.

It may sound strange to make so much turn upon the phenomenon of rhetoric. Obviously the rhetorical tradition concerned itself with only a certain sector of the practical use of language. This is of course true. But when we look at the matter further, we uncover a number of very important aspects. The situation in life which determines the task of rhetoric is that of public speaking. Of course rhetoric can also have applications in private use, for example to the way in which one writes a letter. But the task which is of decisive importance consists of its responsibility for the use of language in public speaking. More precisely, it is concerned with those situations in which a very great deal depends upon effective public speaking because important matters are at stake, and there are threats which can only be countered by words. The primary applications, and therefore the model situations of rhetoric, are the appearance of an advocate before a court and an address to a political meeting. In both cases it is a question of influencing opinion, and in both cases there is explicit conflict with the spread of erroneous opinions: false accusations or harmful political views, which themselves may well make use of demagogy.

Thus rhetoric has a responsibility for matters of vital importance. In a trial a person's reputation is at stake. When one considers the part played in a person's existence by the way he is regarded, the reputation accorded to him, what others think of him and how he is judged, it is not too much to talk, in the case of a slander, of the 'murder of a reputation'. We could well have here a stimulus and starting point for a consideration of the function of language at a much more profound level than is permitted by rhetoric, that of the anthropological and indeed ontological point of view. For rhetoric itself rests upon the fact expressed by Luther in a proverb which he quotes with great approval: 'The world is ruled by opinions.'[57] Just as the judgment people pass on an individual is of decisive importance for him in his public life, so the good of society at large is dependent upon the prevalence of the opinion which is favourable to it.

Of course there are a few qualifications one should make. It is possible to a considerable degree to adopt an attitude of indifference and unconcern towards what people say, in the hope that the truth will ultimately prevail against misrepresentations, or in an attitude of inner superiority which is independent of other people's judgment. But this latter case raises the question of the judgment on which such an independence is based, and which makes us capable of such freedom. This brings us back again to the question of the basis of conviction, a question which in one way and another concerns language. And as far as the good of society at large is concerned, it quite often happens that someone has to do what is necessary without regard to public approval, and comes to have a sceptical view of the validity of public opinion. But once again, this is not to eliminate the question of what one can stand for and be responsible for in this way. Rather, it is posed even more acutely.

But if such vital interests are at stake, every effort to represent them as well as possible is worth while. It is clear that not everyone has the same talent for doing so. The fact that one can talk does not mean that one can also speak effectively in every case and stand up to one's adversary. One might suppose that the person best capable of making a defence before a court is the person concerned. He would certainly not lack a stubborn apprehension of his own interests. The fact that one calls in a lawyer is of course related to the specialist legal knowledge that is required, which a layman does not possess. But this is not the only reason. A very great deal depends, rather, on the intellectual flexibility with which someone can adapt to the situation, on clarity of argument and on the adroit choice of words with which the plea is made, and not least upon the factor of personality, which is so difficult to assess. The latter is not something merely underlying the speech. In many ways it enters into it, into the verbal form, the convincing structure and the way in which it is uttered. To be an advocate on behalf of someone oppressed is an extraordinarily human task. The vocation of carrying out this representative service requires high moral qualities, which ultimately, therefore, are amongst the basic conditions with which rhetoric deals. The same is true in different circumstances of public speaking on political matters. In antiquity the awareness of the difficulty and importance of this task led to people with appropriate talents and education, who had studied the calling of orator, being asked to exercise it. Nowadays, however, a politician either does what he can with the talents he happens to possess or has his speech written by an anonymous colleague in his entourage. This need not be harmful in itself. All the same, such achievements made to order strengthen the suspicion that it is all a matter of technique which is closer to the feel for mass psychology of the advertising agent, fully informed of the results of market research, and to the cunning of the copywriter, rather than to the lofty moral qualities which form part of the traditional definition of rhetoric: 'Rhetoric is the science of speaking well on public matters, to convince people of what is right and good.'[58]

But what can make rhetoric, as an academic artistic theory, capable of effectively achieving the aim of public speaking, that is, to convince the listener? The subdivisions of classical rhetoric derive from the basic theory of meaning and interpretation in the ancient understanding of language. Thus Quintilian gives this definition: 'Every speech consists on the one hand of what is signified and on the other hand of what signifies it, that is of matter and words.'[59] Thus a work of linguistic art uses a synthesis of the content of thought (*res*) and its formulation in words (*verba*). And therefore the *ars rhetorica* is divided into chapters which deal with the *res*, those which deal with the *verba*, and finally the chapters which deal with the relation of the two aspects to each other. The teaching about the *res* is usually dealt with under the headings of *intellectio* (the understanding of the subject to be treated), *inventio* (the working out of the possible ways in which the thoughts contained in the given *res* can be developed), and finally the *dispositio* (the most suitable ordering of the ideas worked out in the *inventio* with regard to the aim of the speech). The part of rhetoric devoted to the *verba* is treated under the heading of *elecutio*: this 'translates the ideas worked out in the *inventio*, and placed in order in the *dispositio*, into language'.[60] And its concern is in fact to formulate them perfectly. Finally, the proper understanding of the *res* and *verba* is dealt with under the heading of the *aptum*, that is the suitability of the speech, both with regard to the inner harmony of its constituent parts and also with regard to the external circumstances, that is, the situation in which it is uttered. This structure, based on a distinction between word and content, does in fact place great importance, within rhetoric itself, on the attention paid to the subject, the *res*. A proper knowledge of the subject is a basic condition of the art of public speaking. The best thing is for the words to arise out of one's own involvement with the subject. Consequently, the finest adornment of rhetoric is that it is to the point. These are rules with which, for example, Cicero defines the relationship between *res* and *verba* in rhetoric.[61] But no more profound consideration was given to the relationship that prevails between them, and therefore it was assumed that the distinction meant that the words, as the outward form, were to a considerable degree autonomous, or could even be dismissed with indifference by comparison with the *res* as the content of the speech. A typical conception is that the content of the speech has first to be worked out and structured, while the form of the language is mere additional clothing and ornamentation.[62]

Of course such a summary of the scheme of categories of ancient rhetoric cannot lead to an adequate understanding of what this form of theory of language in fact achieved. Its true value no doubt lies in the extensive and detailed definitions of forms of speech and figures of speech – that is, what can be regarded as matters of style. By the standard of the questions which arise from the definition of rhetoric and which arouse such lofty expectations, the achievement is a modest one. To some extent this justifies the usual view that rhetoric went no further than matters of form, and taught how to make a speech which was well constructed, but perhaps for that very reason remained without effect. Thus while it touched on the problem of how language should be used in practice, how it can carry conviction – that is, what the conditions are for it to be effective – the rhetorical theory of language failed to carry through its treatment of this theme to a conclusion.

c. Dialectic

While grammar is concerned with language as an abstract system and rhetoric is concerned with it in the form of a concrete individual speech, dialectic addresses itself to language in the process of dialogue. The *dialektike techne* is the art of conducting a discussion, and in the narrower sense the art of disputation. This is the root of the concept of dialectic, which can possess so many and various nuances of meaning. To understand the different point of view from which dialectic attacks the problem of a theory of language, one must pay close attention to the phenomenon of dialogue. Only there is the character of language as an event fully developed. For we are still moving at a fairly abstract level as long as we seek to understand what happens in a discourse solely on the model of an address made by a single person, in which those addressed participate purely in the role of listeners. Of course, on closer consideration this situation is much more complex than this oversimplified and rough-and-ready characterization implies. For a listener as such also participates in the act of speaking. As he listens, his own thoughts (it is to be hoped) take further, in his own way, what he hears. He poses questions or raises objections. What takes place in the mind of the listener is so intimately related to the act of speaking that the way in which he reacts can often be seen in his face and produces a reaction in the speaker. But above all it forms part of the process by which what is said takes effect. For the spoken word is not over and done with the moment the last sound dies away. To this extent, then, listening itself is the beginning of a dialogue, as long as it does not take place without thought, in which case it would no longer really be listening. For listening is an essential condition of anything that is explicitly a dialogue. If the ability to listen to each other is lacking, there is no dialogue, only two people talking to themselves. Dialogue is talking to one another, it is conversation.

But the concept of dialectic is based on a very specific form of dialogue, the disputation. This is done of course in the conviction that the function of dialogue is most clearly expressed in the course of an argument. If the argument goes well, then dialogue is just not marking time – which of course is all that happens in a fruitless disputation – but marches ahead. One word leads to another, but not like an exchange of blows in a fight. Rather, the partners in the dialogue approach each other and go forward together. Statement is followed and taken up by response, and this in its turn calls for a reply. Of course real progress takes place only when the alternation of thesis and antithesis, and new antithesis in its turn, is not like the ball that flies backwards and forwards in ping-pong. Although antithesis is negative in appearance, it is not purely negative, but is a new statement with its own content. And it must correspond to the thesis in the sense that it opens the way for the dialogue to reach a higher level. And this leads to a synthesis, which in its turn may perhaps represent no more than a transitional stage, and be the thesis which sets the process of dialectic on its course again.

Of course one may ask whether this pattern of a fruitful argument which advances knowledge can fairly claim to be the basic model of all dialogue. This depends upon what one understands by the *logos* which determines the nature of the dialogue and which is itself in action as the dialogue proceeds. If one follows the Greek understanding of the *logos* and understands by it the thinking reason, then a genuine argument is in fact the basic model of dialogue, because it is concerned with the process of thought itself, with the autonomous motion of the *logos*. But a phenomenology of dialogue has of course to take into account other aspects which cannot be reduced to this common denominator. There is, for example, the dialogue of psychotherapy or the exchange of words of lovers. The *logos* which prevails here does so in a very different way, for it is more concerned with the words by which man lives, because they touch and move him in his heart. It would be absurd to think of this merely as an underdeveloped variety of the dialogue in which a continuous process of thought takes place. The difference is obvious. Dialogue as a continuous process of thought is concerned with clarifying an issue which does not directly concern those taking part in the dialogue. But when dialogue consists of personal utterance it involves the partners in the dialogue in the subject they have to discuss. Accordingly, in each case the understanding of truth has a different emphasis. In the first case it is truth as the object of knowledge, while in the second case it is truth as the basis of faith. Of course so brief and simple a definition of the distinction cannot be made without qualification. It is only meant to call for further consideration of the fact that the view of dialogue as defined by the concept of dialectic can clearly only refer to a partial aspect of the phenomenon of dialogue. And this affects the problem of a theory of language. If such a theory is based solely on the dialogue represented by the model of the *dialektike techne*, it cannot claim to deal comprehensively with the problem of language. It is even questionable whether it touches upon the decisive issue.

A theory of language as a scientifically developed and methodically applicable art of conducting a dialogue seems to be immediately relevant only to the model of dialogue which is based upon the *dialektike techne*. Here strict rules can be drawn up, which the dialogue has to follow if it is to carry a continuous process of thought to a conclusion. This brings us back to the question of the function which such a theory of language has to exercise. It is obviously not that of bringing the dialogue into being in the first place. The situation here is similar to that of grammar. Grammar, as we saw, simply says what the rules are. That is, it finds them already existing in the actual use of language. Then, of course, it applies them, as consciously accepted standards, to the avoidance of errors of language. In the same way, dialectic can only observe the intrinsic laws obeyed by the *logos* which actually governs the course of a dialogue, then going on to enforce them against any errors of thought which may occur.

This comparison in its turn needs to be qualified slightly. The grammatical rules of language are, by the nature of their application, directly present in language as it is spoken. But the rules of logic are deeply hidden in dialogue as it is usually conducted, and are difficult to observe with precision. This situation changes only when the laws of thought become the object of reflection and are consciously observed in the conduct of a dialogue. Of course in a sense the use of language can also profit from a conscious awareness of its grammatical rules. It becomes as a result more polished, more regular and more varied. This, naturally, may be offset by disadvantages such as the hampering of a living and direct expression. But the relationship between dialectic and the pre-existent and independent conduct of dialogue is a good deal different. The formulation of the laws of thought contains within itself a creative element to a far greater degree than the working out of the laws of grammar. Of course to some extent logical structures and rules can be derived from the spoken language itself. So far the tasks of dialectic and grammar overlap. But to attain the level of a dialogue which is conducted according to strict dialectic rules the first thing needed is a process of dialogue which has the specific purpose of achieving an understanding of the laws of logic. Thus to a certain extent dialectic has a creative function with regard to language. This is not limited to bringing into being a specialist terminology for which a need is first felt, and which then reveals new ways of being conscious of language. The same is true, in no less important a sense, of grammar. But in addition to this dialectic also creates – and this is its main contribution – a way of conducting dialogue which did not exist before. Thus *dialegesthai*, the carrying out of dialogue, and the *dialektike techne*, the art of dialectic, have a reciprocal effect upon each other. Dialectic is derived from the conduct of a dialogue in which the rules of thought are reflected upon and analysed; and then in its turn it has its own effect upon the conduct of dialogue. To put this in a rough-and-ready fashion, by reference to the actual course of history, we may say that without the arguments that Socrates conducted and without the Platonic dialogue there could have been no Aristotelian dialectic, and without Aristotelian dialectic, there could have been no scholastic disputations.

Here we must turn again to the function of a dialectic as a theory of language. First of all, why has dialogue to be carried out as a process of dialectic thought? And what then requires the formation of a theory of language which lays down a standard pattern for the way this thought should be conducted?

Two aspects have to be taken into account here: the limitations and the fallibility of thought.

What is the need for a dialogue which has the purpose of achieving knowledge? In considering this question, the first thing one realizes is the fact that human knowledge is always knowledge from a particular limited point of view. One person sees a situation from his own particular angle and is aware of one special aspect of it, while someone else is concerned with something different. So one complements the other. But each can also correct the erroneous view of the other that his own perception is exclusively valid. And verbal utterances, to an even greater degree, are also subject to limiting conditions. One cannot say everything at once. Things have to be set out in order, and this can only ever be done with particular nuances of meaning, and never in an exhaustive and definitive fashion. Consequently, in any process of thought, every utterance requires to be qualified and complemented by others, so that it is set in its proper place and it leads to a step forward in knowledge. The situation is quite different – be it observed by way of contrast – in the kind of dialogue which was originally excluded from the province of dialectic, and which is concerned with the *logos* by which a person can live. Here there is in fact the possibility of a statement which is final, which does not need to be complemented by dialectic and which in fact is incompatible with it, a statement which says exhaustively all that is necessary, even though, of course, it is just as inexhaustible a task to understand such a statement, to accept it and to let it work itself out in life.

The first aspect we mentioned, that of the need for dialogue to open up and extend our finite and limited knowledge, points to the way the mind is rooted in history as the profoundest cause of the necessity of a theory of language in the form of dialectic. This may be surprising, because logic above all appears to be unhistorical. But this does not necessarily imply a contradiction. Once the involvement with history which penetrates everything that has to do with language becomes conscious, it poses the task of giving a coherent account of certain general conditions of this involvement with history, as basic rules of the way language is to be used. But we must first ask whether traditional logic incorporates a realization of the way thought is historical in nature.

The basic principles of logic were laid down by Aristotle, and logic, in the form in which we find it in his works, is derived from a particular historical way of conducting the process of argument, *dialegesthai*, and is meant to serve as an instrument, an *organon*, for carrying out concrete processes of thought. But it makes the claim itself to represent the conclusion of the continuous dialectic process and to be beyond discussion. Basically, it is no longer of any importance for the instructions which it gives whether the dialectic thought it is discussing is taking place in a real dialogue or not. Only the name dialectic recalls the phenomenon of dialogue. Yet logic abstracts the process of thought as such from dialogue. In this sense thought may be regarded as a dialogue of reason with itself. But even if in fact a dialogue with oneself is characteristic of the structure of the process of thought, a completely new dimension is opened up when a real dialogue takes place, a dialogue between two different persons. Only then is the incalculable and specifically historical element in the process of language experienced. Logic presents a theory of language which is modelled upon the way the thinking of an individual is conducted. A telling real-life illustration of this, albeit completely artificial, could be given by acting out the different steps of thought as they are laid down in the scholastic syllogism, with different persons taking each role.

Traditional logic takes no account of the question of how the universal process of mind is conducted in the universal dialogue which takes place in history, or more properly, which takes place *as* history. The great revolution which Hegel introduced in the understanding of logic consisted of relating it to the dialectic process of history itself. Here the dialectic of thought and the dialectic of reality are conceived of as a single movement. But is it still possible to work out any theory of language on this basis? The question must be posed in an even more acute form. What possibility is there of thought ever going beyond Hegel, if it remains stuck in the rut of the Hegelian dialectic? Instead of working out a theory of language, the task of which would have been to make possible an independent use of language, the philosophy of Hegel fell victim to the danger of tying itself to a fixed and final form of language. Marx, as he vividly expressed it himself, turned the Hegelian dialectic right side up again.[63] But this turning right side up raises even more acutely the question whether it does not result in the end in a *set of rules* for language instead of a *theory* of language.

If the course of history is understood as a dialectic process, then we find ourselves faced with the following problem. Does history speak a comprehensible language, is it actually identical with what happens in language, and can it therefore become the source of a theory of language? Or is there, in spite of the intimate involvement of language and history with each other, a distinction between them which cannot be removed? And is it not then the function of a theory of language precisely to become aware of this distinction and to maintain it?

In comparison with the extending of what happens to language in dialectic to the field of universal history, there is something decidedly beneficial in the sober modesty of traditional logic. Of course it has abandoned the fundamental relationship to life which was to be found in its original concern with dialogue, and which the name dialectic still recalls. It is no longer concerned with the necessity imposed by the historicity of the human mind. It limits itself essentially to another necessity, that resulting from the weakness and fallibility of human thought. Here it exercises the function of a watchdog, keeping a guard upon thought and tracking down errors of thought. In this way it gives guidance in the formation of concrete concepts, in definition, in the exercise of judgment and the process of arriving at a logical conclusion, and specializes in particular in a theory of possible errors.

This form of theory of language proceeds throughout from the fact that human thought faces contradictions. These consist on the one hand of merely apparent contradictions, which can be reconciled by careful definitions and distinctions. In this way apparently contradictory statements can in fact be reconciled with each other by an interpretation which makes the appropriate distinctions. This was the main stimulus to the rise of the dialectic method in early scholasticism: the confrontation of *sic* and *non*, the apparent contradiction of different authorities, and the conflict between *auctoritas* and *ratio*. Secondly, there can be contradictions which are also only apparent, in that they rest upon deceptive assumptions. But since these very assumptions form part of human understanding, the contradictions which arise from them cannot simply be ignored. Kant deals with them in his doctrine of the antinomies of pure reason, and goes so far as to limit the concept of dialectic to a doctrine of transcendental illusion. Finally, there are contradictions which arise through errors of thought. These include genuine contradictions because they ultimately derive from a *contradictio*, that is, from definitions which conflict with each other and which thought cannot reconcile. Such offences against the logical rule that contradictions must be avoided have to be unmasked by seeking the source of the error, so that their lack of validity becomes manifest.

There can be no objections to the value of such a logical theory of language. The question remains, whether it can be of any use in the real problems with which language has to deal.

Dialectic too, in the form of traditional logic, is ultimately an inadequate form of theory of language and points beyond itself. A theory of language which was adequate to justify the use of language over its whole range would need to be able to assist in dealing with contradictions which are not those of formal logic. For the real task of language lies in the sphere of the contradictions which are concealed in life itself.

2. HERMENEUTICS

a. *Hermeneutics and Linguistic Analysis*

Let us turn from the discipline handed down from antiquity, grammar, rhetoric and dialectic, to consider finally another form of theory of language, that of hermeneutics, in order to make clear to ourselves what a theory of language is meant to achieve and what in fact it can achieve. This may seem to be the prejudice of a supporter of one of the two main forms of theory of language which compete with each other at the present day. Side by side with the discussion of the problem of language from the hermeneutic point of view, the approach of linguistic analysis is becoming increasingly important. It was derived from positivism, but has moved in critical independence to a position beyond it. Of course the whole spectrum of present-day attacks upon the problem of language cannot be reduced to these two alternative types without doing violence to the facts. One cannot do justice in this way to the variety of schools of thought and the many aspects of the problem of language. But appearances do make such a polarization appear attractive.

These two ways of looking at language are to a large extent distributed over different geographical areas. This fact rather suggests that their relationship is not that of contraries. Their regional distribution makes it unlikely that the differences between them have been argued out to a conclusion which is adequate to what they contain. For example, as long as different phenomena in the history of religion and the Christian denominations are restricted to different areas, it is a sign that they are determined in part by factors other than those of a purely religious nature. Only when they encounter each other and come into conflict under the same environmental conditions is it possible to tell how far there are real and irreconcilable contradictions, and indeed whether there are any at all. This involvement in the conditions of a particular historical environment, and the limits of understanding which this imposes, are phenomena which play a part in the whole sphere of the problem of language. Thus it is not surprising that something similar also takes place with regard to *reflection* upon the problem of language. Reasons can be found in cultural history for the fact that the tradition of hermeneutic enquiry is more firmly rooted in German- and French-speaking areas. And it is no accident that the approach of linguistic analysis has found a fertile ground above all in the Anglo-Saxon world, thanks to its dominating tendency to an empiricist attitude to reality. And yet the factors which have to be taken into account here cannot be reduced to so simple a distinction. The ideas of linguistic analysis, which have spread above all in the Anglo-Saxon sphere, are of course due to a very large degree to emigration from the German-speaking area. But to argue for an inner affinity between the ominous forces which drove the men of the Vienna Circle to emigrate and the hermeneutic mode of thought would be to jump to conclusions on the basis of purely partial symptoms, and would simply show that one was ensnared oneself by false hermeneutics. In the meantime there has been a considerable change in the German-speaking area in the direction of linguistic analysis. But this in its turn should be attributed not simply to the change in political circumstances, but to a shift in the centre of gravity of a general kind in the sphere of cultural interests.

There seems to be one solid reason for the polarity between

the different approach to language in hermeneutics and linguistic analysis, and that is the concern of the former with the humanities and the latter with the natural sciences. But even in this respect they overlap, so that such a simple formula is not permissible. Certain groups who adopt the point of view of hermeneutics passionately support the division between the humanities and the natural sciences. But this is no justification for tying hermeneutics definitively to the concept of the humanities (which is considerably open to question), in order to play off against it the alleged primacy or exclusive claim of the scientific method. As long as one persists in defending this antithesis, one is still under the spell of the hermeneutics which one is opposing. A reinterpretation of the situation which has given rise to the distinction between the humanities and the natural sciences, and which of course must still be taken into account, calls for a comprehensive attempt to understand it. Consequently one cannot escape the task which hermeneutics sets itself. Mathematics, for example, is in a sense an extreme case of the humanities, the sciences of the intellect; on the other hand, it is the least applicable to history. This shows the difficulties that have to be taken into account. Thus the view has gained ground that the separate existence of the two ways of thinking about language, with virtually no connection between them, is simply a consequence of the inadequate state of the discussion. If the relations between them are examined more closely, it is possible to perceive, in spite of all the differences between them, a good deal of common ground in the questions they pose.

An example of a tentative in this direction is the article by Karl Otto Apel, 'Wittgenstein und das Problem des hermeneutischen Verstehens' ('Wittgenstein and the Problem of Hermeneutic Understanding').[64] In this article a concern for the problem of understanding still dominates the way the relationship is defined. But Hans Albert finds a different kind of common denominator, from the point of view of the critical philosophy of Karl Popper, between the approach of hermeneutics and that of linguistic analysis. He regards hermeneutics as 'a continuation of theology by other means' and dismisses it from the first.[65] Basically, therefore, he gives preference to linguistic analysis: '. . . in the comparison between the two schools, the investigations of linguistic analysis, often so pettifogging, can usually be compared to their advantage with the ambitious but often vapourous language games of the hermeneutic school.'[66] But he regards linguistic analysis, as a result of the way it limits itself to the question of meaning, as restricted as much as the hermeneutic approach to what already exists, with the result that both are trapped in conservative descriptivism, which avoids the task of criticism. He concludes: 'We are faced, therefore, both in linguistic analysis and hermeneutics, with a more or less concealed "positivism", although both regard themselves as superior to "vulgar" positivism . . .'[67]

Thus if hermeneutics is understood as the attempt to develop a theory of language with the widest possible horizon, it will be able to accept what is valuable in linguistic analysis, and give weight to it in dealing with the problem of language. And this will effectively set it free from the suspicion of concerning itself uncritically with what already exists. The discussion that follows will therefore deal with the question whether the principle we have just laid down, that hermeneutics should be understood as a concern for a theory of language with the widest possible horizon, is justified.

b. A Theory of Language with the Widest Possible Horizon

We are justified in understanding hermeneutics in as wide a sense as this by the original meaning of the word *hermeneuein*. The root meaning is speech as such: to speak, to say. The meaning develops from this in three main directions: to put into words (express), to expound (explain) and to translate (interpret). The link between these three divergent meanings is a concern for the understanding *of* language *by* language, that is, the achievement of understanding, either by a statement which is to the point, an explanation which makes the meaning clear, or an accurate translation. The same intention is present in each case: to enable language to achieve its full effect in carrying out its function. Thus hermeneutics does not set out to add anything to language, but only to remove what prevents it from being effective. It tries to repair the breakdowns which interfere, either within language itself or outside it, with the process of conveying understanding, which language itself is meant to bring about.

The word *hermeneuein*, therefore, both in its basic meaning and in the way it is used, points towards a theory of language with the widest possible horizon. The way hermeneutics is usually defined in practice, as a theory of understanding, points in the same direction. A theory of understanding is required only in so far as language, for any reason, is incapable of what it is intended to achieve and which it normally achieves quite straightforwardly. Thus it is a theory of how breakdowns in language can be overcome. For this purpose it must be a theory of language of the widest possible horizon, the reason being that it has not only to study the causes of breakdowns in language, but also the conditions for the untroubled exercise of language. For ultimately language can be helped only by language: incorrect or false statements by correct and relevant statements; obscure statements in need of explanation by an exposition which makes them clear; a misleading exposition by an accurate interpretation; a statement in a foreign language by translation into a language that can be understood; and a translation that distorts by a faithful version.

One may not find these indications sufficient to remove all doubt about whether language can really be helped only by language. Perhaps it may be thought somewhat difficult to accept the curious doubling of the process of language which is expressed in the concept of a 'theory of language'. For any theory is obviously expounded in the form of language, and a 'theory of language' might be thought reminiscent of Münch-hausen's attempt to pull himself up out of the bog by his own pigtail. But even if one cannot brush aside this doubt, and consequently maintain a sceptical attitude to the various possible forms of a theory of language, the basic facts which I shall now go on to discuss must be recognized. I hope to show that the closer one's starting point is to the basic situation of language, the wider will be the scope of the task which faces a theory of language.

c. Taking Language for Granted, Disorders of Language and the Criticism of Language

That there is any need of a theory of language at all is due to the questionable nature of our dealings with language and to our dependence upon help with language. The reliability of language, and the difficulties which we encounter with it, are experiences which are clearly related. These difficulties appear all the greater to us because they are disorders in something which we take for granted – in something which can be taken for granted, moreover, in the full sense of something which takes care of itself, about which we really do not have to worry, and which on the contrary takes away the need to worry, supports us and helps us. Thus 'help with language' sounds strangely tautological, because language itself is an instrument of help, by the very fact that we can take for granted that it is at our disposal, a ready availability which it furthers itself. In order to live at all we are very much dependent upon this living space which can be completely taken for granted. It is an indispensable condition of any ability to encounter what is incomprehensible and cannot be taken for granted, the only basis on which we can come to terms with it and so extend the range of what is accessible to our understanding.

The term 'mother tongue', so extraordinarily rich in associations, expresses more than the mere fact that it is normally our mother who gives us language when she first teaches us to talk. The phrase 'mother tongue' ought also to remind us that in every process of communication life, love and language are still an indivisible unity. In it, it is as though the child's journey out of the womb is continued. For the process by which man becomes human is by no means concluded with birth. It is no mere metaphor but a living reality, that the mother tongue in which a person first awakes to consciousness is the second mother who bears him, providing his life with the power of growth and protection as he grows. By teaching her child to talk, a mother in a sense hands him over to language as to a second mother, who endows him with the security of what can be relied upon. But just as conflicts necessarily arise in the relationship with the real mother, so they arise too in the relationship to language. And they are only satisfactorily overcome when the exchange leads in the end to the restoration to language of the right kind of reliability.

Because we are now approaching the problem of the theory of language in so extreme a fashion, from the point of view of the fundamental interpenetration of language and life, we become aware of issues which are extremely universal in nature. A precondition of all knowledge is the shock which is caused by what is not understood, the terror at something strange which provokes questions and thereby initiates the decisive movement in the process of understanding. Even when what is strange and has not yet been mastered does not so much cause uneasiness as a disturbance and a threat, but rather provokes curiosity, here too something reliable is now called into question. This uncertainty may be feared or it may even be longed for. Scientific ethics include a readiness to declare that something that has mistakenly been thought reliable is wrong, regardless of one's own fears and wishes, and to maintain the thirst for knowledge and the search for understanding, even in the face of appearances. Here the necessary criticism is strictly speaking not aimed directly against certain parts of reality, but always against certain ways of interpreting and evaluating it. And even where, as in economics or politics, criticism is aimed at specific material circumstances, such as the catastrophic food situation in the countries of the third world, the inadequate safety precautions in a factory or the ludicrous relationship between defence expenditure and the money allocated for overseas development, the direct object of the criticism is always the state of mind which calls such circumstances into being or accepts them without thought, excuses them or even supports them. To this extent one can say that all criticism, being a process of language, is also a criticism of language. That is, it is a criticism of a particular interpretation of reality, of some fixed pattern of language or other, or else of an ideological glossing over of the facts.

But we ought not, by a one-sided choice of examples, lose sight of the fact that the structure of the language which expresses such a criticism can vary greatly, depending upon the situation. It is not always that of a blatant unmasking, aimed at destroying the object of critical attack. Even with questions of practical action in the social sphere, the situation is usually not so unequivocal that only one point of view and only one opinion is right. In general, the acquisition of scientific knowledge has the great advantage that it can be tested experimentally and demonstrated mathematically. In this case, the scope for conflicting opinions is relatively small. Yet even here, looking at the matter as a whole, there is a characteristic distinction to be made between the way natural science looks at things and the commonsense way in which reality is regarded in daily life. The latter is of course not superseded by the scientific description, and the two views are not mutually exclusive. Naturally, with regard, for example, to the structure of matter, the scientific view must be maintained in its criticism of what can supposedly be taken for granted on the basis of appearances; but it must also be maintained against scientific theories which are regarded as certain. But however much theories which are proved wrong must be discredited, the rightness of the commonsense view for our everyday dealings with things is not thereby disproved. This points to the fact that there is a justifiable plurality in the horizons which language envisages. And anyone who cannot distinguish between them is a victim of a false and foolish brand of criticism.

These observations on the different ways in which what is reliable can be criticized and called into question cast light in a number of ways on the problem of a theory of language. Perhaps the most difficult thing with regard to language is to stand back from it sufficiently to question critically what is taken for granted in it. For one of the basic functions of language is to supply something that can be taken for granted. Only on this basis is it possible to call into question at all what is taken for granted. To make language itself the object of radical questioning would necessarily mean stepping outside it, yet this seems to mean abandoning the possibility of any critical questioning at all. One must be aware of this profound dilemma in every endeavour to establish a theory of language. Reflection upon language can only take place by means of language itself. This corresponds to the fact that in all his endeavours to obtain knowledge, man cannot escape from the conditions of humanity. The criticism of language *in a particular respect*, either in regard to one or other of its formal structures, or in regard to one or another concrete form of spoken language, makes great demands upon the ability to concentrate upon background phenomena which attract the least notice because they are taken for granted. Yet the task of a *comprehensive* criticism of language is much more difficult, and from the methodological point of view presents immense problems. It requires a theory of language which, from an understanding of the basic conditions of all language, can derive criteria for carrying out a criticism of language in individual aspects, in order to diagnose the causes of the disorders of language, and also to point the way to a therapy which can cure them.

d. Language as a Living Process

That we can only reflect upon language by means of language of course represents a difficulty. But in other respects it is an advantage. The wider the horizon in which a theory of language is considered, the closer is seen to be its relationship to life. This assertion will no doubt seem arbitrary until the evidence for it has been demonstrated. Discussions of the theory of language not infrequently give the impression of being remote from life and barren. Although a comprehensive theory of language has hitherto existed in tentative form, it has never been carried to a conclusion in the systematic and detailed way – comparable to a fugue in many parts – which alone can make clear its relationship to life. But the right to expect that a theory of language conceived in comprehensive terms should have a very close and detailed relationship to life, seems to me to derive from the very fact that such a theory of language transcends the distinction between theory and practice. The more it takes into consideration the whole living process of language, the more it already participates in this living process itself. Because it studies disorders of language and disorders in life, in order to seek out their causes and tackle them at the root, a theory of language cannot restrict itself merely to instructions by way of help in the use of language. As an exercise of the responsibility for language, it will itself strive to achieve a language which is of help to those who use it. It serves itself as a training for the living process of language. We might express this by saying that the more fundamental the way in which the task of a theory of language is understood, the less it gives the appearance of mere theorizing about language. Thus the aim is to make practical use of language in a helpful way. For language succeeds in developing its utmost resources when by language one person sets another free to make a wholesome use of language. Because such a theory of language sets out to deal with the acute disorders in language, it can only succeed in providing this kind of help if it prepares the way for language that is reliable in a new and purer sense.

If the form of a theory of language is to be derived from the widest possible range of language as it is actually used in life, the tension must be maintained in every case between the active use of language in *speaking* and the quasi-passive use of language in *listening*. I use the expression quasi-passive because, although the emphasis here is on the experience of receiving language that is spoken, this receiving implies a specific kind of activity. That is, to someone with an open mind what is asserted will be immediately obvious, while someone who has different preconceived ideas is unconditionally required to open his mind to it. Language can be properly understood only when the full range of what takes place in it is appreciated in this way, and both aspects, the way language comes into being and what comes into being through language, are linked in a unity. Usually a theory of language is limited to a single aspect, that of the way language comes into being through the interplay of language as a formal system and its subject as the content of spoken language. Similarly, hermeneutics is usually restricted to the other extreme, to the understanding of certain manifestations in language and the overcoming of the difficulties which they present to the understanding. But speaking and listening are complementary aspects of a single situation. Speaking is basically orientated towards listening, and listening to speaking.

To speak is to cause someone to apprehend, and to listen is to apprehend. Because the two aspects of the one event of language are complementary, in the concrete use of language they are inseparable. To a certain extent speaking originates in listening, in an apprehension already made. And only when the listener allows himself to be heard is it clear that he has apprehended anything. Thus the relationship between the speaker and the listener is not a simple one, like that between the launching-pad and the target, between which language takes its flight and transports items of information. This mechanical conception must be completely transformed. We should rather say that language brings the speaker and the listener together in the same place. It draws them together, or at least it ought to. It works for an understanding in which the speaker and the listener do not merely share odd items of information, but, albeit through the medium of such a partial degree of mutual assent, learn to understand each other and ultimately achieve a common mind, a harmony.

But the desire to see the phenomenon of language as a whole should not lead us to an over-hasty and polemical rejection of the concept of information. In information theory it is usually only a partial aspect of the phenomenon of language which is under discussion, and this is an important aspect which should not be dismissed as insignificant. Moreover, one is drawn into the whole vastness of the problem of language the moment one really attempts to examine thoroughly all that is implied by information.

It is this wide range of the use of language in life, which we characterized by the polarity between speaking and listening, which first brings to a head the problem that prevents a theory of language from remaining what it is usually considered to be, a theory which is never put into practice. Of course one must explicitly warn against an uncritical acceptance of the implication in the phrase 'a theory which is never put into practice'.

It does not merely imply condemnation, and cannot be used without further ado as a standard of criticism. One of the basic conditions of scholarly and scientific work is to be bold enough on occasion to create a theory which cannot be put into practice. We must also realize that we do *not* know, or at least often cannot know in advance, how much practical relevance a particular theoretical understanding may come to have. We must therefore explicitly guard against the misunderstanding that to endeavour to construct a theory of language with the widest possible horizon implies even the slightest degree of contempt for the laborious detailed work of technical studies in hermeneutics and linguistic analysis, or for the immensely taxing abstract methodological examination of the problem of language. Anyone who lacks the patience to make short and preliminary steps forward in his understanding can rightly be suspected of uttering mere empty words. If a theory of language has a disciplinary function, this lies not least in warning us against confidence tricks in the use of language, and in urging upon us a modest and conscientious, precise and respectful use of language. Anyone who nevertheless goes on to attempt the construction of a comprehensive and accordingly fundamental theory of language must pay particular attention to this warning. And the more experience he has of this task, the more willing he will be to admit how much his own attempts in this respect are open to question. But he must not be afraid to take the risk, provided vital problems are really at stake.

Keeping to the polarity between speaking and listening, we see that this vital complex of problems is focused upon two questions which are inseparably related to each other. How can a significant use of language be achieved in our present age? And how can a common mind amongst the people of our time be achieved through language? Instead of elaborating these questions at the moment, I shall content myself with illustrating each by a quotation. Of course my choice is somewhat arbitrary. For the problems which these two questions raise are so complex and fundamental that the literature on them is almost inexhaustible. In his essay on 'The Problem of Language' the Swiss philosopher Jean-Claude Piguet writes: 'What is questionable at the present day is neither the positive properties of language, nor its functioning, but the relationship between language and what is to be said. For one may attempt to describe or define the nature of language in a scientific manner, or else one can limit oneself to analysing the role of language in the human sphere. It is possible to adopt both approaches with regard solely to the fact that something is said, and without regard to what requires to be said. But the greatest and most difficult problem of language at the present day is not concerned with the relationship between the act of speaking and what is said, but between the act of speaking and what should be said. For the crisis of our time is not caused by our inability to speak, but by our no longer knowing what we should speak about.'[68] An American linguistic philosopher, Benjamin Lee Whorf, stressed the necessity of linguistic work with regard to the urgent problem of understanding in the following words, which exactly describe the responsibility of hermeneutics: 'Wherever agreement or assent is arrived at in human affairs . . . this agreement is reached by linguistic processes, or else it is not reached . . . The more complicated and difficult the matter, the more such knowledge [of linguistic processes] is a distinct aid, till the point may be reached – I suspect the modern world has about arrived at it – when the knowledge becomes not only an aid but a necessity.'[69]

3. THE DIMENSIONS OF THE PROBLEM IN A COMPREHENSIVE THEORY OF LANGUAGE

A comprehensive theory of language must pay attention to

what is at stake for life itself in the use of language. What is the cause of the disorders in language which represent a disorder in life? What comprises a wholesome use of language which can give an adequate account of life and the threat to it? And how is it to be achieved? In order to break the task down into its different dimensions, we shall adopt as our pattern an outline of the way language is manifested as a living process. If we make our starting point the polarity of speaking and listening, the basic situation can be expressed in the simple formula: I am saying something to you. In itself this is an empty and meaningless phrase. But it would have a concrete sense if it were used to shake someone out of his inattention and to provoke him into realizing that he was being spoken to. In such a case the phrase would be given meaning by the situation in which it was spoken, and this situation would include what had already been said and what it was concerned with. But here we shall use it merely as an empty formula, in order to consider the possibilities it offers, the requirements it assumes, the dangers it conceals, and the extent to which we can look for any way out of our difficulties in this framework.

But to divide this short formula into its component parts will lead to an accurate knowledge of the partial aspects of what takes place in language only if we examine not merely the external, grammatical syntax, but as it were the internal syntax of the living process itself. Thus we must not attempt to isolate what is, in the literal sense of the word, 'concrete', that is, what has 'grown together' in the living process of language. Rather, we must take account of the way every aspect is intimately linked with every other. Then we shall be able to look at the different aspects separately, but only with some difficulty, stumbling constantly upon traces of the links between them.

a. *The Speaker as the Subject of the Process of Language: The Authority to Speak*

What we have just said is immediately applicable to the subject of the process of language, the person who speaks. This person cannot be regarded in isolation from what compels him to speak and makes him capable of speaking, but only in relationship to it. From where has he derived what he says? In what way are the fact that he speaks, the content or the manner of his statement already determined by the listener to whom he addresses himself? What question or demand has the listener already put to the speaker in order to make him speak? One could go on indefinitely asking such questions, but it is already clear that the 'I' in the formula is not to be thought of as an individual isolated from every context. It must be regarded from the point of view of what conditions it: the language traditions on which the speaker depends or from which he has broken away; the historical and social circumstances which have formed his life, or perhaps restricted and deformed it; the experiences which have made him what he is or his lack of experience, or at least of assimilated experience. And of course in all this one must take into account the unique way in which he has been formed as an individual by natural tendencies, inherited characteristics and the events of his life, including the limits circumstances have placed upon the development of his personality, and what, on the other hand, he has been able to make of what has happened to him. Although there is considerable scope for a variety of responses to the demands made upon a person, in any given case the number of possibilities is very limited. But however much the range of statements the speaker has at his disposal may be restricted by circumstances, and however powerfully he may be manipulated by anonymous forces, as a being possessed of language he is never wholly absolved from all personal responsibility for language when he makes use of his right to speak.

In every conceivable modification, the basis of the use of language is the two-way movement of apprehension and utterance, comparable to the systole and diastole of the heart. Ultimately, it is identical to the double movement of all human life, turning in on itself and going out from itself. If reflection upon the process of language is to dwell on the 'I' as the subject of speech, it must pay attention to the breakdowns which occur in this alternation of apprehension and utterance at the origin of the process of language. Is the apprehension erroneous or hampered? Is the utterance inadequate to what the speaker has apprehended? Is he saying something which he cannot vouch for, which he has never experienced, and which is perhaps contrary to his experience? Within the sphere of what a person intends to say or what others expect of him, what he endeavours or even neglects to say, he displays to others and experiences himself an inability in many respects. This phenomenon raises the question of the power which brings apprehension and utterance into harmony with each other and which enables someone to utter what is fit to be said and good to listen to. Thus every observation about the 'I' in the process of language boils down in the end to the question: What ultimately gives authority for the use of language?

b. *The Act of Utterance: Responsibility*

If one now turns from the speaker, the subject of the statement, to pay special attention to the act of utterance, the form of the verb itself shows how closely linked the two are. It is governed by the subject and takes the tense appropriate to the subject and set by it. The verb as it were binds the sentence into a unity, in that it is dependent in every possible direction and at the same time makes the other elements of the sentence dependent upon itself. It is the heart of the sentence, without which it would have no life. But it becomes precisely defined only by virtue of the other elements of the sentence. Thus the saying does not take form until not only the subject is present but the object as well, determining the content of what is said, with the indirect object, the person addressed, determining to whom the statement is directed. Not until they are present does the verb become the central link which binds all the rest together in a coherent statement and qualifies it. The 'I' now appears as the 'I' who is *speaking*, the 'you' as the 'you' who is *spoken to*, and the object as that which is being *spoken about*. Here all the relationships are drawn together into one. Thus if one spotlights the act in which the spoken utterance takes place, the first question which urgently arises is whether and in what way everything which the act of speaking draws into a single complex in fact fits together. The first thing, then, to be considered is what modification the act of speaking undergoes in *this* particular situation, by taking place with *this* particular content between *these* particular persons: whether it takes the form of conveying information, instructing, addressing, promising, forbidding, complaining, exhorting, comforting, or whatever it may be. But the first thing to be asked would be whether the act of speaking, under whatever modification, was in place in the actual situation.

There are a number of possible causes of breakdown here in the process of language. For example, somebody may say something which he has no right to say to the person he is speaking to. Or else what he says may be out of place in this situation. Or else the situation is such that it does not require anything at all to be said, but calls for something quite different. Of course nothing should simply be condemned as a breakdown in language with regard to the situation simply because the statement is felt to be disturbing. It may well be that an extremely disturbing statement is the only one appropriate to the situation, while a statement which is timely and appropriate in a trivial sense and gives no offence at all can be hopelessly inadequate to the situation and completely lacks what is necessary. Whether justice is done to the situation cannot therefore be judged solely by the preservation of what already exists. It may be that the only utterance appropriate to a particular situation is one which brings about a fundamental change in it. Of course in a sense every statement changes the situation. Even an utterance which leaves everything as it was when the precise opposite is required is not without its consequences, if only to increase discouragement and resignation.

If we look at the act of speaking in this way we become terrifyingly aware of the fact that things can happen through the process of language which cannot be reversed. Opportunities can be missed for good, though they can also be seized at the right moment, with unsuspected long-range effects, putting to rights what is dangerously disordered. Here we focus again upon the aspect of the responsibility for language. In the face of the breakdowns which can overcome the responsibility for language, the aid to language that is required should be discussed principally in the light of this question: What helps us to understand the situation and see it so clearly that the very word it requires comes at the right moment with the power to set it to rights?

c. The Object of the Statement: the Challenge to Understanding

In order to understand the process of language, it is of particular importance to look at the function of the object of the statement. Many lines of discussion of the theory of language cross at this point. Where the main concern is with what is being said, interest is usually concentrated upon the relationship between the form of language and the content of language, while the relationships existing in the process of language which go beyond this remain excluded. But if the principal concern is with the *process* of language, the preoccupation with the personal relationships that occur within it is usually so great that the question of the content of what is said is largely suppressed. Attention is restricted to the phenomenon of one person addressing another and comforting him, promising him something, and the like, so that the impression may be given that a simple informative statement about a particular matter is somehow a deficient form of utterance.

But for a right understanding of the personal relationships in the process of language it is necessary to realize that language does not directly unite the speaker and person or persons to whom he is speaking. The encounter always takes place within the context of a particular matter. Of course this can happen in very different ways. In the discussion of an historical matter or a technological task, those who are taking part in the process of language can meet in the object of discussion. Because they are wholly involved in the matter, they completely set aside their self-consciousness and their personal interest in one another. But even when personal relationships are dominant, as for example in a conversation between friends, the encounter normally takes place through the medium of some matter which is being discussed between them. Even if the discussion is dominated by reflections upon personal affairs, these too are turned into an objective matter of discussion. And even in the intimate conversation of lovers, when almost every objective element is replaced by a pure outpouring of one heart to another, even such a direct statement and pledge of love partakes in a certain sense of the nature of an object. It is as though a meeting place were set up which enclosed the lovers and provided a place where they can live. For the love which they express and pledge transcends the present moment and what is already a reality in it, and forms, as a promise and a standard, a kind of counterpart to the direct personal relationship.

Yet in no case, not even that of a statement concerned purely with its object, does what is uttered lose all connection with the whole process of language. Of course there are good reasons for shading out relationships of this kind and, for example with the intention of carrying out a critique of language, for studying only the relationship between the form and the content of language: whether the statement is meaningful, whether it accurately represents what is intended, whether it is well worded, and whether the wording is free of inappropriate overtones, etc. There is a wide field open here for investigation, all of which would be of value for a theory of language: whether appropriate categories are used, to what extent judgments can be tested, how the limits of what can be said are defined in each case, and so forth. But once the attention is directed towards the process of language as a whole, the relationships which exist between the matter being stated, the speaker and the listener make themselves felt. Thus, for example, who makes a statement can effect how much weight it carries. Or there may be reasons for carefully guarding against introducing this point of view. Again, one may point to the fact that every statement is meant to exercise an effect upon the listener in some way or another. This often sets up a complicated relationship between the content of the statement and its intention. The way the material and personal components of a statement are intertwined in the process of language must never be allowed to be a symptom of a lack of objectivity, although this possibility must always be taken into account. But basically what is said, the person who says it and the person to whom it is said are always related in a complex way and, of course, depending upon the circumstances, to a varying extent.

Against the obstinately held view that this assertion is only about something peripheral and fortuitous, a mere external appendage of the content of the statement, we would advance the following consideration. The object of the statement is of course not simply present in tangible form. Rather, it is uttered; that is, it is presented in the form of language. What is present in the process of language is not an object manifesting itself directly, but one mediated through language. And we must not conceal from ourselves the importance of this fact by taking as our model nothing but primitive examples of statements in which the thing being spoken about is always there to be pointed at, like the illustrations in a child's first reader. The specific capability of the statements of language is to express in language what is not directly present, and to make present what is not, or not yet, manifest in itself. And the extreme case is that it is capable of bringing to utterance what cannot be other than spoken and can never be made present in any other way.

The fact that the object of a statement exists in the form of language is a source of the commonest disorder of language. For example, errors or lies can creep in, so that unintentionally, or even on purpose, the use of language can result in deception. A statement may be true in itself, and yet subject to misunderstanding; or it may be so imprecise that it cannot with certainty command assent. But the true function of language would be lost if in using it the very hazardous element of the challenge to understanding were wholly excluded. The somewhat bold expression 'the challenge to understanding' is used to sum up an extraordinarily important matter which I have already discussed.[70] The purpose of a spoken utterance is to set the listener into action in the direction of understanding. It attributes to him a productive participation in the statement in his own mind. It does not fulfil its task any better, for example, the more it reduces the listener's need to think. What language can and ought to achieve is made all the more clear, the more a statement provokes thought.

d. The Person Addressed: Mutual Understanding

In the schematic sentence 'I am saying something to you',

which we took as our model in feeling our way towards the different dimensions of the process of language, the statement is ultimately characterized as directed towards a listener. However, for a statement to be explicitly addressed to a particular listener is by no means the rule even in the case of the spoken word, let alone in the case of printed publications. In public speaking, or within the sphere of influence of the mass media, the listener is largely or completely anonymous. Yet the point of view of the final goal of the process of language cannot be ignored, any more than that of its starting point. Even a writer who, not troubling himself about the public, convinces himself that his words can wait until their time comes, is submitting himself to the judgment of his readers in the future. But even if the conceptions one has of one's audience are not taken into account at all, we must affirm that every utterance of language is of its nature potentially subject to the judgment of those who hear it, and it is they on whom one is making demands, they whom one influences, and their criticism to which one is subject.

The disorders which have to be considered in this aspect of the process of language are caused when the intention of the speaker in his use of language comes into conflict with the intention of the listener in using it. For he could not be a listener if he did not also make use of language. Thus he is not a *tabula rasa*, but an extremely complex context into which the statement is uttered. And this effect is of course multiplied in the case not of an individual listener but of the numerous listeners to a sermon, or even more to a statement on the radio or the television, or of the unknown circle of readers who read a book, or who will read texts which are translated from their contemporary context into a strange one, into other ages and civilizations. The fruitful but dangerous tensions which arise from the discrepancy between the text and the context are the principal occasion for the endeavours of hermeneutics. But if we ask which gap between speaker and listener is the hardest to bridge, and where the obstinate causes of resistance are to be found which prevent a common mind being reached, we are left with the problems of mutual understanding which we cannot always solve to some extent by careful interpretation and patient translation. The real impediments are those caused by a determination not to listen, and by the impotence that comes upon us when we do not have at our disposal words which would be adequate to the real needs of life and which could do them justice and help us with them. Here the problem of mutual understanding becomes a problem of power and authority.

e. Verification

The four main aspects into which we have subdivided the process of language, by following the grammatical structure of the model sentence 'I am saying something to you', have shown us more than merely the different elements of the process of language, the speaker as its subject, the act of speaking as such, the content of the statement and the person addressed. At every stage of the analysis we came upon the basic constituent processes of language, together with the disorders of language that accompany them and the aid to language required to overcome them. The main aspects into which we were able to resolve the inner structure of the process of language are expressions of what actually happens and is at stake in it, that is: the authority to speak, the responsibility of language, the challenge to understanding and the achievement of mutual understanding. These essential elements make it clear that the process of language is not just one living process amongst others. Rather, it is the meeting point and essence of what is ultimately at stake in life. What has a person – this particular person – to say? Does he make use of what has been given to him to make known? And what use does he make of the fortunate chance that he is a human being, the possessor of language? How does he exercise his responsibility for the word in any particular situation? What kind of challenge to understanding does he invite and what kind of challenge to understanding does he make? What sort of communication takes place in his life? At how profound a level does he achieve mutual understanding? To what extent and to what degree does his life convey life? These brief hints, which, by comparison with the reality of life itself, are inevitably no more than formulas, show that the relationship between the process of language and the process of life itself is so close that in the end both are ultimately regarded as a unity.

Is it still necessary to guard against the foolish misunderstanding that this is to identify life with language, and existence with talk? The reverse should already have been made clear, that language is included in life, and talk in existence, as integral factors. For in the process of language it is ultimately life itself which is seeking utterance. And for this reason it is life which is at issue in every case in the process of language. It should be obvious that this is not an invitation to spend most of one's life talking. Since language is so intimately associated with life, something of the necessary reverence for life should be carried over to the way we use language. Our choice of speaking and silence should show that we are aware of the connection. When something is precious it must be guarded with particular care. And in bringing to light what is hidden in life, and is as easy to wound as it can wound itself, we should act all the more conscientiously and cautiously.

The authority to speak, the responsibility for language, the challenge to understanding and the achievement of mutual understanding – these four key phrases represent the main dimensions of the problem of a comprehensive theory of language. Let us now attempt to focus our enquiry even more closely, and seek the one basic source from which these fundamental processes of language well up and flow in different directions. We must consider the following assertion: these four aspects are developments of the way in which, and the extent to which, the process of language is concerned with truth. Verification and, concentrating solely on the negative aspect, falsification have been put forward by logical positivism and its developments as methodological concepts for the critical determination of whether statements are meaningful. The dominant view of truth here, however, is a very narrow and questionable one, taking the form of what can be established empirically by sense data or what is logically demonstrable and valid. The task of working out what things are true in the different verification and falsification theories and the range in which they are valid, and of incorporating them into a comprehensive theory of language, is one which is unquestionably to be accepted even with regard to a theological theory of language. But under no circumstances must we allow the concept of verification to be restricted to this use. It must be related to the question of truth as it is posed in life and through life itself. It is no accident that a consideration of the process of language as a whole should find at its heart the concept of truth, so that the task of a theory of language is concentrated upon the concept of verification. For the truth is at issue solely and exclusively when reality is being dealt with in language. But wherever language is doing what it is its nature to do, its ultimate obligation is to the truth alone, and it is by the truth that it must be tested. Thus a theory of language with the widest possible horizon has consequently to define the task of verification in an equally comprehensive way.

The key phrase *the authority to speak* reminds us that the task of verification becomes acute at the very origin of the process of language. A person who makes use of language must be true himself, so that he speaks the truth in the most demanding sense. 'Every man is a liar'[71] – this points to a profound problem in a theory of language based upon the process of language. Here the question of the verification of language is replaced by the question of the verification of the person. He possesses language, but in a highly ambiguous fashion. In every case he finds himself in possession of the truth in a sense that this is the precondition of his changing the truth into a lie. But he repeatedly finds himself, and his fellow men find him, behaving as a being possessed of language and yet constantly in conflict with what this definition implies. However much this situation may be qualified, or however radically it may be interpreted, it cannot in any case be denied that man who is not identical with himself, who contradicts himself, in fact exists. Thus the authority to speak would lie in the speaker's attaining to the truth, the truth which sets man free to use language without self-contradiction. By contrast, the key word *responsibility* is a call to be aware of the situation of language and of what it requires. The key phrase *the challenge to understanding*, which we used to cast light on the function of the content of a statement, leads to the simple realization that what we have to say can be straight away defined by saying that we have to speak the truth. Every stage of the criticism of language therefore serves to ensure that whenever we speak we are speaking the truth. Finally, the key phrase *the achievement of mutual understanding* reminds us that the aim of language is to make the community between men in the complexity of life a true one.

The failures of language are the risks, obscurities, and disorganizations which do not allow the truth to come about in the process of language. And the help which language grants can ultimately only be that which helps the threatened and damaged process of language to return to the truth and to serve the truth.

If we dare to take a further step and characterize as decisively as possible the concept of truth as it is related to life, the definition on which we light may sound extremely banal, but the longer we think about it, the more significance it takes on: The one thing that is true is love. In concluding the discussion of dialectic, I said that 'the real task of language lies in the sphere of the contradictions which are concealed in life itself'.[72] This is an appropriate commentary on the statement that the one thing that is true is love. To base a doctrine of language on this statement is to move towards a theological theory of language.

CHAPTER IV

Basic Questions of a
Theological Theory of Language

I. THE SPECIAL CHARACTERISTICS
OF A THEOLOGICAL THEORY OF LANGUAGE

The assertion that *general* considerations about language lead to a *theological* doctrine of language indicates how much our theme has involved us in the issues of fundamental theology. The impression might be given that our intention is to base the theology of the word on a theology of language. This would be a contradiction in terms, in so far as it would be completely contrary to the purpose associated during recent decades with the slogan 'the theology of the word'. From that point of view, such an approach would result rather in the liquidation of theology of the word. But in any case the expression 'theology of language' is not at all what is meant by 'a theological theory of language'. I dare say that cheap theological journalism, ever in need of sensation, would like to see another addition to the series of 'theologies of . . .' to provide a few more headlines. But I assure them that I have no intention of proclaiming a 'theology of language'. Nor does the expression 'based upon' seem to me to express adequately the relationship between general reflections upon language and a theological theory of language, nor the relationship of both of these to the whole of theology.

On the other hand it is essential for a theological theory of language to maintain close contact with general considerations about language and to make fruitful use of the latter for theology as a whole. For its task is to reflect upon the mutual relationship of the language of the general experience of the world to that of theology; to test the necessity and truth of the latter against the preponderance of the former and its claim to be autonomous and self-sufficient, and in this way to initiate a mutual process of criticism between the two forms of language. This conception of a theological theory of language removes the suspicion that it is concerned merely with isolating from the rest of the world of language a dialect which it seeks to preserve in being, however difficult this may be. To do that would be a contradiction of the function of language, which is to communicate. It would be precipitate, to say the least, to reject the conception of a *theological* theory of language altogether, on the false grounds that it is seeking to establish a distinctive sacred language, not subject to the general criticism which is applicable to language, or – a negative view which is perhaps nearer the mark – as if it were simply seeking to justify a despairing lapse into a trivial ghetto language. To concentrate entirely on the task of a theory of language in general terms, without taking up the specific problems of particular fields of language, would be a profitless affair. It would be to ignore the real need for a theory of language. This need is always produced by a *particular* use of language and the problems it raises.

a. A General and a Particular Theory of Language

The way general and particular issues are related in this case raises problems which can be mentioned only briefly at the moment. There is some justification for the fear that theology might be reduced to part of a discipline with precedence over it and including it, and that it might be subject to outside criteria. In this way it would be deprived of its autonomy, a general theory of language being accorded the task of judging to what extent this autonomy is possible and of defining its limits. The history of the relationship between theology and philosophy or, if we follow the older and less restricted understanding of philosophy, the relationship between theology and knowledge as a whole, is overflowing with examples of this kind. On the other hand theology would be losing something essential if it tried to escape these problems, as far as there is any possibility of doing so successfully at all.

In a certain sense, however, it is true that theology is subject to *general* criteria. This is not because it has been negligently subordinated to the requirements of scientific and academic knowledge. If this were true, theology would be subject to postulates derived from outside, and could reject their authority if it so chose. Of course one must take care that theology is not overwhelmed by inappropriate academic postulates. But to do so would itself represent an act of self-criticism on the part of theology, based on scientific and academic principles, even though it might well, in any particular case, result in a dispute about the misunderstanding of scientific and academic knowledge as such. Yet it is an essential element for the existence of theology that it should be ready, without qualification, to defend the cause of Christian faith in the open forum of the whole experience of the world. This is not something which is an optional extra to Christian faith, remaining external to it. It is rooted in its very nature. For Christian faith includes the certainty that it concerns everyone and can be uttered in a way comprehensible to everyone. Theology rests upon the conviction that the corresponding process of the confrontation between Christian faith and the whole experience of the world, demonstrating that it is comprehensible and valid for everyone in the sense of the challenge to understanding appropriate in this case, does not obscure what is specific to Christian faith. On the contrary, it makes its distinctive nature even more obvious.

These remarks must be clarified. What do we mean here by scientific and academic knowledge? And how can the aspect of the attribution of understanding in matters of faith be reconciled with the claim that the Christian faith is comprehensible and valid for everyone? Above all, the pattern of the general and the particular which underlies this discussion must be considered more closely. The conception of a system of knowledge, which like Porphyry's tree branches off into general and distinct species, but is held together by an inner necessity, is an oversimplification. This is not just true of theology. The process of the search for knowledge is subject to constant movement and change. The different forms it takes vary from many points of view, such as the range of its subjects, its methods, the kind of questions it asks and its relationship to practice, to mention only a few of the main aspects. Of course there can be such a thing as a general theory of language which is relevant to all the particular forms of a theory of language, at least in the sense that the latter must come to terms with it. This applies, for example, to what we said about grammar or dialectic. Similarly, it is also possible to think of a general hermeneutics. But these examples illustrate the fact that the universality attributed here to any one discipline is true only in certain respects. Paradoxically, it is due to some special feature of each discipline. Of course the relevance of grammar is extraordinarily wide. Everyone who uses language critically must be thoroughly familiar with it and must be guided by it. But in another respect it is an extremely specialist discipline. But the more widely the attempt is made to make actual use of a particular theory of language from the point of view of its general relevance, at the expense of a concentration on specialist aspects, the more questionable it becomes whether the task can be of any value or is realizable in any meaningful academic sense. The tendency to increasing specialization is a powerful driving force in scientific and academic work. For one achieves academic competence only by detailed knowledge. And yet one cannot submit to this law unreservedly. Quite often the progress of knowledge and the usefulness of detailed study depend upon the power of synthesis, upon whether one is able to proceed from the particular to the general. But this does not invalidate what we have already said.

Consequently a theory of language of a general kind, intended to be comprehensive in its range, must be based upon concrete issues and concerned with specialist aspects. Otherwise it runs the risk of becoming empty and saying nothing, the more general it becomes. Moreover, a general theory of language conceived of in comprehensive terms can stimulate and advance further discussion only if it adopts a decisive attitude to the basic questions which it is bound to face. It must not commit itself to the ideal of a neutral formalism, or, as usually happens in such a case, give the mere appearance of neutrality. Here again, the special aspects of a theory of language have to complement its general application.

These considerations show how wrong it would be to subordinate a theological theory of language to a general theory of language, as though it were a special case of the latter. From this decisive point of view, one might say rather that the theological theory of language goes further towards a comprehensive theory than is usually the case with any other form of theory of language. Because it calls attention to basic questions, and, because of its concern with them, places issues of detail in a very broad context, one might expect it to make an important contribution to a general theory of language. This also explains how, when we analysed the process of language, the attempt to focus upon what is ultimately at issue brought us close to a theological theory of language.

The sceptic might ask how strictly objective this focusing process was, and whether there is any evidence for the suggestions that occurred to us as we made it, and he is entitled to an answer. We would point out that the study of the matter itself in fact *suggested* the relationship between a general and a theological theory of language. Whether and to what extent anyone may wish to take the trouble to consider and examine the matter further, testing it from the point of view of a genuine 'scepticism', depends, as always in such cases, upon the personal attitude which leads him ever to undertake such a consideration. This, then, does not do away with the call for a demonstration of evidence. But one can perhaps anticipate agreement with the statement that the problems with which a theory of language seeks to deal are concerned with a matter which is capable and worthy of objective discussion in the broadest terms.

The distinction which is relevant here between matters of form and matters of content is subject to the same qualification which we made with regard to the pattern of the general and the particular. The charge made against hermeneutic studies, that they restrict themselves to formal matters, unquestionably touches upon a serious danger. But if we are aware that the concept of the formal goes far beyond its usual limitation to external form, and if we then pose the question of form in correspondingly radical terms, it brings us in fact to fundamental questions of content. The analysis of the brief sentence 'I am saying something to you' demonstrated this. Consequently, reflection upon the language of theology lags far behind the point to which it ought to be taken if it does not break through artificial restrictions and become a consideration of the subject matter of theology itself.

b. A Theological Theory of Language, and Theology as the Theory of the Language of Faith

At this point we must consider a further distinction without which it is not possible to outline the structure and task of a theological theory of language. Such a theory of language is not relevant solely to the language of theology, that is, to the problem of forming adequate theological concepts and judgments. The tasks of a theological theory of language of course include this, and yet it is not exclusively concerned with theological language, as a particular specialist language. Its principal relevance is to the language of faith. For this provides theology with its object, and poses its task. Theology is determined by it to such an extent that there are good reasons for describing it as a whole as the theory of the language of faith. But if one also accepts that the language of faith in its turn is meant to provide help in the form of language, that is help for life in the form of language, the impression grows that a theological theory of language is concerned with a remarkably complex subject. We can only do justice to it, then, if we do not separate what belongs together, but pay special attention to the links within this complex subject. I want to emphasize only a few of them.

If theology as such is a theory of the language of faith, one must then ask what the specific task of a theological theory of language may be. At first sight it seems a disadvantage to define its tasks in such fundamental and wide-ranging terms that it is difficult to draw a line between a theological theory of language and theology as such. The natural wish for a definition which prescribes limits is disappointed, and its purpose threatens to become so vague as to be lost. The problems here are similar to those which occur in the relationship between fundamental theology and theology as a whole. This is no accident. A theological theory of language has very close links with tasks undertaken by fundamental theology. At the very least, it is an important ingredient of fundamental theology. If we take this into account, we can describe the situation as follows: a theological theory of language is required as a separate theological undertaking when theology faces a crisis of language, but none of the existing disciplines offer adequate opportunity or possess suitable tools to deal with the things which these problems bring to the fore. For all traditional theological disciplines are affected by the crisis in the same way. In order to overcome it, it is necessary to make a new approach to the common theological task, which, if it is successful, will make all disciplines aware once again that they belong together, and require them to co-operate effectively. Thus a theological theory of language as a separate undertaking is both a symptom of crisis and an emergency measure, with the aim, if possible, of making itself superfluous.

c. The Language of Faith

Theology accepts responsibility for the language of faith, but does not create it. The language of faith comes first. The Bible, in particular, comes first in the narrower historical sense that it was written before Christian theology came into being. Throughout its history Christianity has always regarded itself as dependent upon the Bible as the source and norm of the language of faith – even though there have been great differences in the way this dependence has been understood and used. This fact, now as always, is characteristic of Christian devotion. Directly or indirectly, it is nourished by the vocabulary of the Bible. This, however, is not enough to make perfectly clear what is meant by the language of faith. A further fact must be taken into account. The word fixed and preserved in the Bible cannot claim of its own to be the language of faith. It does as a matter of fact take undisputed and absolute precedence. But even when a biblical statement is taken as it stands and used in a particular situation, the very fact that it is used and applied in this way means that to a certain extent it is being rewarded. For in a particular situation it carries special implications. And by this very fact it is no longer the dead language of the past, but the contemporary and living language of faith.

But the most appropriate use of the language of the Bible is when it enables us to produce our own language of faith independently. This process expresses two complementary facts: faith depends upon the Bible for its language and so for its life. But the Bible shows faith how to use its own words. The category of exposition or translation is hardly adequate to describe this process, unless it is understood in a much broader sense than is usual. It seems inadequate even to the process of language that takes place in a sermon, and still more for Christian hymns and prayer or for quite informal Christian utterances. Only when this free use of the language of faith is achieved does it become really clear why a theory of the language of faith is necessary. It is particularly illuminating to consider why the Bible, with the incomparable power of its language, cannot and is not meant to be understood as the model for the language of faith, a pattern book of devout phraseology, entirely excluding a free use of language. It consists to a large extent of narrative and consequently, although it can be retold, it cannot simply be repeated. But something essential would be lost if the Bible relationship to history, which is the determining element not merely in the narrative parts, but also in those of its other statements which relate to particular situations, were treated as of no significance in forming the language of faith. And the remainder of the Bible would be reduced to nothing if all connection with its own time and environment were removed from biblical language, to enable it to be directly repeated in any age.

These facts are familiar, and they lead to an important conclusion. The language of faith is not something distilled out of the ordinary language of the world and separate from it. The Bible itself is a living proof that the language of faith is of its nature deeply rooted in the language of the world. And here 'the language of the world' is a formal expression for the confusion of languages that is found in the world. It covers the whole complexity of what cannot of itself be uttered on the basis of faith, but within which the language of faith, accepting and rejecting it, responding to it and contradicting it in all kinds of ways, takes living form. Only within this encounter with the language of the world, and indeed only by this means, can faith be uttered at all. And the language of faith exists only because of this encounter.

d. The Principal Scope of a Theological Theory of Language

This conclusion helps us to define the principal scope of a theological theory of language. Let us first define it negatively. A theological theory of language is not a set of rules for language which is restricted to providing practice in the phraseology and vocabulary of a particular language. Of course such a thing exists within Christianity on various levels: certain denominational languages or devotional languages which breathe the atmosphere of a particular period, or the languages of ecclesiastical schools of thought which can be recognized by certain shibboleths, or the transitory languages of theological tendencies. On all these levels the extremely unpleasant phenomena of indoctrination, intolerant censorship and almost ludicrous imitation can be found. Of course we shall not let such distortions obscure our understanding of the legitimate practical and sociological necessities which result in the formulation of the Church's creeds, the establishment of theological schools of thought, the maintenance of a common language of faith on the basis of tradition and the prevention of theological language from lapsing into confusion. On the other hand, we should not be too quick to suspect others, intolerantly, of imposing their ideologies, or to accuse them of a repressive censorship of language. For it is possible for something like a genuine consensus to exist. If one looks in church history for something other than scandals, it is clear that on many occasions a consensus has actually existed; the gift of a common language enjoyed in liberty. And whatever else a theological theory of language must do, it must provide this.

But we ought not to ask too much of it in this respect. It is not its purpose to act directly as the language of faith or to provide it. Living devotion and its genuine utterances are not derived directly from theological reflection. One cannot as it were think oneself into belief and teach oneself its language. If the contribution which thinking and learning can actually make here is to be a fruitful one, it depends upon processes deep down in life itself which are beyond control. These precede the reflection of theology upon them. And theological reflection, if it is properly conducted, constantly points back to them. Without such a link with experience theology, as the theory of the language of faith, becomes empty. But this relationship of dependence does not mean that the function of theology has been demoted. Theology as a whole, and, with its specific responsibility as fundamental theology, a theological theory of language have to ensure by their critical vigilance that the language of faith never ceases to exist in the form of an encounter in the midst of the confusion of languages present in the world. The two poles of this process of language do not exist as independent entities, which as such can be disentangled from one another, and only afterwards related to one another as a supplementary task. They are only what they are in their relationship with each other. Thus the language of faith is the dialogue of faith with the experience of the world. And the language of the world as such is a confused and concealed dispute about faith. It is the concern of a theological theory of language to bring to light this inner polarity in the language of faith and by so doing to maintain it in its purity. In this way faith, in accordance with its nature, can remain in contact with the experience of the world, and the fact that it is a dialogue can provide the standard for the critical testing and the exercise of the language of faith.

2. CRITERIA OF A THEOLOGICAL THEORY
OF LANGUAGE

If a theological theory of language is to provide this service, the criteria which it has to follow must be more precisely defined. This will also serve to make clearer what its specific nature is, for a reflection upon the *language* of theology now takes its *subject matter* as its theme.

a. The Loss of Polarity

The necessity of precise material criteria is obvious from the fact that the status of the language of faith as we have described it is threatened. This danger is something which is inseparable from the language of faith, because it exists only in an encounter with the confusion of languages in the world. To extricate itself from this encounter would bring it only an apparent security. In fact it would fall victim as a result to an absolutely fatal danger. If the language of faith ceases to be in dialogue with the experience of the world, it has effectively become the language of unbelief. The salt has lost its savour and is no longer good for anything; it can be thrown out and trodden under foot. If the language of faith draws apart from the world and consequently becomes deformed in itself, it deserves to be abandoned completely to the world. Thus the threat against which a theological theory of language has to guard with a critical eye is misunderstood if it is described as a danger to the balance between faith and the experience of the world. The cure for this would be an equal dose of each. This view gives rise to the muddled idea that the language of faith can be heard to excess, and that it can be corrected, at least from time to time, by a one-sided overdose of the experience of the world. If one is content with superficial answers, this may seem to have something in it. But it misrepresents the true situation, because it thoughtlessly identifies the language of faith with a particular existing tradition of language and likewise regards the experience of the world as an entity unambiguous in itself, which can be formulated independently of the language of faith and can simply be added to it. If we take seriously what we have elucidated concerning the element of polarity in the language of faith, the threat to it can be resisted only within the experience of the world; that is, face to face with the cause of the danger.

The loss of polarity, which deforms the language of faith, can manifest itself under various appearances. We can typify its extreme forms as secularism and – if a neologism may be forgiven – religionism.

It is perfectly clear that secularism, with its emphatic doctrine of one kingdom, destroys the polarity which is at issue in the language of faith. This is of course not all that takes place in the different forms in which secularism manifests itself. A more rigorous interpretation would show this. Such an interpretation would have to take into account on the one hand the justifiable polemics which give secularism its emotional force. And on the other hand it would have to pay attention to the suppressed elements in it which enable us to see that it manifests itself in a different way from that to which it lays claim.

By religionism we mean the formal establishment of a religious attitude which acts as though it were self-sufficient, in isolation from the experience of the world. Of course its claim to do so cannot be taken seriously, since in practice it always amounts to nothing more than the attribution of a special status to a certain sector of the reality of the world, with which the rest of the experience of the world is contrasted. Consequently, a religionism of this kind remains firmly in the grip of the secularism to which it is opposed. Either a particular area of worldly reality is directly claimed to be the domain of religion, or else religion is wholly reserved for the inner life of the soul. In this way, the language of religion becomes a provincial dialect. That to which it is opposed, and to which it adopts either a purely negative or an indifferent attitude, remains something external and accidental to it. It has no essential significance for it as a partner in a dialogue.

We must, however, guard against writing off, on the strength of this description, situations to which it apparently seems to apply, but which it is not possible at all to understand in this way. Some people naïvely suppose that the secularist criticism of religion is unreservedly good for faith. And so they attack every form of religion which is clearly defined in a set language and a firmly established pattern of life, and deny the relevance of the inner life of the soul. But they are ignoring the fundamental fact that the language of faith cannot do without the language of religious tradition.

But the fact that the language of faith is inseparable from the language of religious tradition does not mean that no distinction can be made between them. One of the essential tasks of a theological theory of language is to interpret the tradition of Christian language on the basis of this distinction. Briefly this means, in negative terms, that it is by no means necessarily to the advantage of the language of faith for religious language in general to be in common use. That God is spoken of in one way or another is no guarantee that he is spoken of in a proper and adequate way. Talk about God is not a neutral foundation on which the Christian language of faith can be built as a superstructure. Rather, the language of faith is a struggle for the right use of the word 'God'. And what is true of this central issue of religious language radiates out from it to illuminate the whole field. Religious language as such is not the language of faith. Even Christian religious language does not guarantee, without qualification, a usage and an understanding which are in accordance with faith.

b. Jesus as the Embodiment of the Criteria of the Language of Faith

The Christian tradition sees Jesus as the embodiment of the criteria by which the language of faith is judged. Of course the understanding of Jesus and the way in which he is the criterion of the language of faith has been a subject of dispute from the first. But this does not do away with the necessity for the language of faith always to take account of Jesus. The fact that this task is always a subject of dispute is related to what we said about the polarity intrinsic to the language of faith. The constant reference of the language of faith to Jesus forces it into the dialogue of faith with the experience of the world. Consequently, this all-embracing process of language cannot attain any definitive final resting point within history, in which the language of faith would be out of danger, uncontested and beyond dispute. Nor can there be any standpoint outside one's own participation in this process of language from which one can decide upon or resolve the dispute as a neutral arbitrator. Thus the hermeneutic situation with regard to the language of faith is, so it seems, precarious and uncomfortable. The claim to truth can only be put forward here on condition that it is permanently challenged. And as the ultimate argument for its verification, there remains only the frank identification of the subjectivity of the believer with the subject matter of faith. These circumstances show with the utmost clarity the specific connection between the language and subject matter of faith.

In turning now to propose a number of main criteria for the language of faith, with reference to the figure of Jesus, I am aware of the following difficulties. The statements as I word them cannot make any claim to be absolute and exclusive, as though they could be phrased only in this way and not otherwise. And even if the suggestions I make could assume a wide degree of assent, they would not be beyond dispute. Neither of these considerations make these criteria any less usable. For whatever divergent views may be advanced against them, in the nature of the matter their only place is in the content formed by the aspects we are going on to discuss.

A number of links with what we have already mentioned in the general analysis of the process of language suggest once again some considerations of method. Are there indications of an illegitimate influence by a general theory of language upon theology? Or was our general analysis of the process of language secretly shaped by the theological points of view we were to adopt later? Were our conclusions merely what had already been presupposed? Or are there genuine correspondences here between two distinct approaches? Are there really issues raised in the context of the problem of language which lead us on to a theological theory of language? Are there good grounds for affirming that the subject matter of theology has an astonishingly close affinity to the theme of language? And if this is so, how are we to interpret such correspondences and connections? I mention these questions so that at least I am not exposed to the charge of concealing them. Their treatment must follow other lines than the usual ones of a distinction between nature and grace, or reason and revelation. But this is not the proper place for so wide-ranging and ambitious a task. We must now content ourselves with the observation that some fundamental criteria of a language of faith show a connection with fundamental aspects of language as such.

A. TRUTH

If the language of faith is to be in harmony with Jesus, then it must have an unreserved obligation to tell the truth. We must at once add, in explanation of this, that we are referring to the truth which concerns the whole man; the truth by which one can live and on which one can rely in life; the truth which can be apprehended only by a comprehensive process of cognition which is similar to the total living act in which man and wife 'know' each other;[73] the truth to which the startling phrase 'to do the truth'[74] is appropriate. But we must guard against a confrontation between different concepts of the truth, which might give the impression that the truth was not an indivisible unity. It would be absolutely unthinkable to concede, in the name of the unified concept of truth which is based upon life itself, that one does not have to be very meticulous about the truth. But in the light of the truth which comes as a gift and a challenge from Jesus, a preoccupation with partial truths, an obstinate digging-in behind dead ortho-doxies, or a malignant and life-destroying concern with truths cut off from their context in life, are unmasked as propaganda on behalf of falsehoods posing as truth.

We have stated that this is a criterion for the language of faith, that it must give unlimited scope for the truth. We must make this statement more precise by emphasizing two things. Nothing can credibly be proposed as the language of faith which cannot honestly be defended by the person who speaks. One cannot sacrifice the subjective awareness of truth to an alleged objective truth, Still less can the question of truth be left in abeyance for the sake of any consideration, however easy to understand from a human point of view. This honesty, in which the speaker accepts personal responsibility for what he says, must be coupled with the decisive will for the truth which seeks for clarity in regard to what has to be said, and is not afraid of revealing uncomfortable facts. These remarks may seem trivial. But honesty and a will for the truth, in the strict and all-embracing sense in which these are criteria of the language of faith, are not so common that we need pay no attention when someone says that the language of faith stands and falls by them. And when those who are beginning the study of theology sometimes express a concern that loyalty to the language of faith can sometimes threaten to lead to dishonesty, one can only reply that the courage to take the risk of coming to grief with the language of faith is a condition which is in the interests of faith itself.

And let it be noted that truth as the criterion of the language of faith is something that applies to language as a whole. When we gave a general analysis of language we asked *what* was to be said. And our answer was the simple affirmation that one must speak the truth. For truth is the empire of language. But we did not make this the starting point of our present argument, applying a general demand for the truth to the language of faith. Rather, it is in the nature of faith itself that it should so strictly require truth to be the criterion of the language of faith. The power of language is obviously so great that faith will not tolerate a use of it which does not submit to the discipline of truth.

B. LOVE

If the language of faith is to be in harmony with Jesus, then for the sake of truth, it has an obligation to love. It would perhaps be more accurate to say that it has an obligation to truth for the sake of love. And yet to link them in this way makes one acutely aware of the problems raised by the relationship between truth and love. Everyone knows from experience that there are situations in which for the sake of love, one may not perhaps speak untruth, but where nevertheless the truth cannot be uttered. And the opposite view is also based upon experience: that for the sake of truth love must sometimes be suspended, and perhaps even hatred must be propagated. Truth has sometimes to be ruthless. At any rate, truth and love do not seem to belong together without reservation. Love can threaten truth and truth can threaten love. Nor would I be wholly truthful if I did not feel bound by other reasons than those of the truth alone. There is something in all of this. And for this reason the connection between truth and love is a firm one only when one has an obligation to love *for the sake of the truth.* This demonstrates the meaning of the truth to which the language of faith has an obligation for the sake of Jesus. I said of it that it is a reliable truth by which one can live. But the general analysis of the process of language also led to a concept of truth related to life, and I ventured to sum it up in the expression, which sounds rather banal: The one thing that is true is love. By way of explanation I added the phrase which concluded the discussion of dialectic: the real task of language lies in the sphere of the contradictions which are concealed in life itself. The combination of these points of view pointed towards a theological theory of language. Were we already assuming here a theological idea, such as is expressed pre-eminently in the statement 'God is Love'?

Be this as it may, the statement 'The one thing that is true is love' is hardly unequivocal in itself. To discuss it would bring all kinds of horrors to light and destroy many illusions. And what would it mean for truth to be so closely linked to love? The answer one might expect is that love as a *command* is the essence of truth related to life. How else is it possible to speak of love? Love is action. When it is expressed in words it is an act which is commanded, the commandment of love. We are of course aware of the dilemma: Can love be commanded at all? Can a commandment of love produce love? Surely it is only possible for love to be called for when it is already there in any case? But we are also aware that love is by no means expressed in language solely in the form of a command. As we all know, there are endless stories to be told about love. It is inexhaustible, and the need for love cannot be appeased. But love is clearly more deeply involved in language when it is being spoken, when one person speaks love to another. One may say that love is really wordless, justifying this by the statement that it is action, or perhaps, even more radically, by the statement that it is inexpressible. But this is not the whole truth. How meagre the love between a man and a woman remains when, although there are no external limits to it, there is an inability to pour out one's whole soul in the exchange of words. What riches love can unfold through spoken communication! But we can trace the connection between love and language at a still deeper level. The process of language itself is, in its basic intention, an exercise of love. A tiny child to whom no one speaks, who is not drawn into the community of language, is destroyed by lack of love. The keenest expression of the destruction of community is that people no longer speak to each other. And it is a marvellous sign of reconciliation that people speak to one another again. Indeed words must act themselves as means of reconciliation, as words of reconciliation. Harmony comes into being through love mediated by language.

Relating this to the figure of Jesus, we can say that love is the criterion of the language of faith, and that no detailed proof is necessary for this statement. We could find evidence of it in the tradition about Jesus, as we have already tacitly done in speaking of truth as the criterion of the language of faith. And we shall content ourselves once again with merely pointing out that the correspondence in fact exists: love as the criterion of the language of faith is in accordance with what can be said of language as a whole.

C. FAITH

But why must the language which is to be in harmony with Jesus and which, for the sake of truth, has an obligation to love, be the language of faith? The simplest way one can put this is to say that it is because truth is distorted and love fails. Accordingly, the language of faith is the revelation of truth as the imparting of love. Answers such as these, given in brief formulas, need to be defined more closely by the unlimited complexity of the experience of the world. This is true in the first instance of the description of the ways in which the truth is distorted and love fails. But it is also true of the task of proclaiming in the face of this distortion and failure the meaning of the revelation of the truth and the imparting of love. Of course the opposition here should not lead us into treating it as an unrelieved contrast between black and white. The experience of the world must make itself heard with all its nuances, its heights and depths, its horrors and its marvels. In so far as it represents a distortion of the truth, the honest and passionate search for truth and the value of partial truths should not be despised or ignored. And similarly the experience of the world which represents the failure of love should not be caricatured by being restricted to the gross and obvious cases. Rather, all the moving and entrancing elements in human love must be present if the necessity of the language of faith is to be credible. Otherwise we should have an absurd attempt to plead the cause of faith at the expense of truth and love, and the very opposite effect would be achieved, a destructive caricature of faith. Only by taking into account the experience of the world in an undistorted form can the language of faith impart a love which is above the world but – or better still, and therefore – totally related to the world.

For this, however, it is necessary to have recourse to what is utterly concealed and beyond our control, that is, to God. But honest recourse can be had to God only when this is done in the name of the reconciliation of the world with God. And therefore nothing in the experience of the world which has come to be uttered must be suppressed and treated with violence by the word of reconciliation. We must return again to what we have said about polarity in the nature of the language of faith. When we spoke of the criteria of the language of faith under the headings of truth and love we pointed to their correspondence with what is true of language in general. What is the situation here, where the polarity in the nature of the language of faith is more evidently the criterion by which it is judged? Here too, in fact, the correspondence with a basic situation in language is evident. It is of the nature of the language of faith that, in relation to the complex variety of what is directly and tangibly present, it asserts the presence of what is hidden, in the sense of a presence which can only be communicated by language. As we have repeatedly shown, the true power and function of language is that it gives expression in words to what is concealed, not in addition to and alongside what is perceptible by the senses, but 'in, with, and beneath' the phenomena of reality. This ancient formula of sacramental doctrine is very appropriate here.

But there is another point of view from which we must consider further what we have said about polarity in the nature of the language of faith. How are we to use this aspect as a criterion? This leads us to the relevance of the distinction between the law and the gospel for a theological theory of language.

c. The Law and the Gospel

A theological theory of language is important in fundamental theology because theology is pre-eminently concerned with words. First of all, as an activity which reflects upon and seeks to give an account of the language of faith, it is a complicated linguistic process in itself. It is consequently concerned with every concrete form of Christian utterance: with the tradition of Christian language in its canonical and non-canonical forms, together with what has been the context of these texts in the past and the present context in which faith has to be vindicated. To put the matter even more pointedly, *the subject matter* of theology itself *is* words, not only because the gospel in fact takes the form of words, which is obvious, but also because it is not possible to encounter the content of the gospel other than as something conveyed in language. Within the confusion of languages in the world, God's love for the world can only be imparted in words and belief. The gospel corresponds, in the way it consists of words, to the way in which the world as man experiences it is determined by language. This is true regardless of the fact that in certain respects the gospel is in contradiction to the language of the world and so is contradicted by it.

But the gospel does not take the form of isolated words existing alongside a supposedly naked reality. The only way in which it can be uttered is by referring to the reality which in some form or another has already been brought to utterance, the reality which makes such complex claims upon men and is so passionately disputed amongst them. This process of language, which has already been going on for an immensely long time, and in which the experience of the world is concentrated in an infinite variety of forms, is essential to the word of the gospel. To use one of the most difficult terminological abbreviations which exist within theology, this process of language represents the interpretations of the law which are uttered in language of great confusion and numerous meanings. The gospel as such builds up on them, which is how it comes to be articulated. By so doing, however, the gospel first makes clear what the law is. Only then is the law understood as such at all, and its virulence, but also its limits, made manifest. Thus on the one hand the gospel supersedes the law, while on the other hand it gives it a force it hitherto lacked.

The doctrine of the law and the gospel which is given here, in no more than the briefest outline, is of decisive importance for a theological theory of language, above all for the following reasons. It indicates how to relate the language of faith to the experience of the world in the appropriate way.

Anyone who allows himself to be guided by these indications of the way the subject matter of theology should be understood, and theological decisions taken, will have impressed upon his conscience as a theologian the need to work constantly to maintain this interpenetration of the language of faith and the experience of the world, and so to play a conscientious part in the continuous formation of the language of faith. A theological theory of language which is based upon the distinction between the law and the gospel avoids two dangers. On the one hand, it guards against preserving the gospel as a timeless entity isolated from the experience of the world. This would be to turn it into a pseudo-law. On the other hand, it avoids applying the Christian word directly as a law to the present experience of the world and turning it into a programme of political action. This would be to turn the law into a pseudo-gospel. In both these false forms the language of faith loses the character of a dialogue with the experience of the world. Either it flees from it or falls victim to it. In either case it ceases to be the language of faith.

3. AN OUTLINE OF A THEOLOGICAL THEORY OF LANGUAGE

Since what takes place in the language of faith presents a parallel to what is at issue in the process of language as such, it is appropriate in working out a theological theory of language in detail to take as our model the four aspects of the problem which resulted from our analysis of the process of language. We represented the main aspect by the key phrases: the authority to speak, responsibility, the challenge to understanding, and the achievement of mutual agreement. In working out a theological theory of language it would be necessary at each of these stages to give effect to the tension and distinction between the law and the gospel. This would also be to take account, in a way appropriate to the language of faith, of the different aspects of the problem of verification. Let us make this clear in a short sketch.

a. The Authority to Speak – the Letter and the Spirit – Experience

As far as the *authority* to use the language of faith is concerned, we are dependent upon the language of faith spoken previously and spoken to us. This is true of language as a whole; we have received it by its being spoken previously and spoken to us. And the same is more or less true of everything which we are able to say. One need only try to imagine being without everything which we owe to the language we have received. What kind of power of speech of our own would we have left? Entirely dependent upon our own resources, we would be like fish out of water. We would largely lose, with the language which forms our environment, our own living use of language, and if that went, it would certainly not be all to go. Thus we should not be surprised that we are dependent upon the language of faith spoken previously and spoken to us. Much more remarkable is the fact that such a tradition of language has come down to us at all. The original authority to use the language of faith is a rare thing, as history teaches us.

But a reference to the traditional language of faith is not a sufficient answer to the question of our authority to agree with it and to make use of it. Nor can this problem be reduced to the technical question of how to understand and use the traditional language aright, and how to expound and interpret texts, so that they can inspire what we have to say ourselves, and our words are effective and to the point. If we were to allow our conception of what the authority to use the language of faith means, and how it is obtained, to be governed by the achievements of the crafts of exegesis and homiletics, we would not even acquire the necessary degree of fear of the monstrous task involved, far less the courage to undertake it.

All due respect to this craft! In general one could only wish that theologians were better masters of their craft, instead of hankering after things that seem more interesting to them, with the consequence that they have a dilettante knowledge of everything, including theology. But the courage to be modest requires in the case of this craft a knowledge of the wider context beyond its own limited sphere. The authority to use the language of faith is a matter of *experience*. Language arises only from experience. And only in this way can the language we have received become our own language.

And there is also an opposite experience, corresponding to the structure of polarity in the language of faith. This can best be described by the two Pauline concepts of *the letter and the spirit*. But it goes further than the usual application of these concepts to the question of how the written word can once again become a living thing, and how the spirit dormant in the letter can be awakened, so that one is not merely dealing with a dead letter. This is itself a process which is far beyond what can be achieved by technical means. No one who cannot contribute his own vitality to his treatment of a text is likely to be able to draw life from it. The rule 'To him who has will more be given' certainly applies here. But the dialectic of the letter and the spirit is concerned with how not one or other particular aspect of life, but life itself, should be the subject of experience. In its most extreme form, in the conflict between death and life, the issue is the decision about what is really and truly life. Anyone who – to use Pauline language – does not know the power of the law to kill, also has no true knowledge of the life-giving power of the spirit through the gospel.

Not long ago it needed courage for a theologian to use the despised concept of experience. Nowadays the sparrows on the rooftops tell us that for a theologian it is experience and practice that matter. Now it requires courage to contest the erroneous view that it is enough to appeal to 'the material of empirical facts' and, by going on to snatch at experiences of any description, to give the appearance of a theology concerned with practical action. But what really matters is to bring to light in *all* experience the issues which are essential in matters of faith. That is, we must not rest content with the mere letter of experience, but be open to the experience of the spirit in which, because it is a matter of life itself, the issue is one of *death* and *life*. This is the only way the authority to use the language of faith can be attained.

b. *Responsibility – Binding and Loosing – the Experience of Freedom*

The exercise of the *responsibility* of language in matters of faith draws our attention to the relevance of the situation. The state of affairs usually described by expressions such as 'conditioned by its time' or 'contemporary relevance' shows that the situation of language is highly ambiguous. Of course every statement of language is conditioned by its time. One must be aware of this. But one can expect of it that it should not be wholly subject to the power of time, but in one respect or another should break the bonds imposed by its own time and set itself free from its imprisonment in the present moment. Only then can it freely contribute anything to the present moment, and be completely committed to what it gives us and to what it demands of us. What we should be able to expect from the power of a statement is not least that it can make time available to us and bring about the beginning of a new time by changing the situation. The same is true of its contemporary relevance. Only words which apply to the present time and which are appropriate to it, that is, which are timely, can be of any real help. This must not be confused with a contemporaneity which is slavishly subject to the present and which, because it so readily keeps step with the present time, can be seen on closer examination to leave everything as it was. Quite often, what really has contemporary relevance is in conflict with its age.

Considering further the problem of the way a statement of language is related to its situation, we find that the authority to speak is manifested as the freedom to speak, as the courage which dares to say everything, as the power which seizes upon the *kairos* of the word. There is no finer expression of this than the Greek word *parrhesia*. Thus the reference to experience extends to *the experience of freedom*. This is manifested in the way one exercises responsibility for words. But in addition it makes it clear how the relationship to the situation must affect the words themselves if they are to be as it were on the target, and fundamentally change the situation.

Following the structure of polarity in the language of faith, one could say here that the Christian word is always uttered in the *duality of binding and loosing*. It is irrevocably enmeshed in what exists, what is required, what has happened and what is missing. But it is an incredible liberation from the enslaving forces, the guilt and the anxiety, which are so powerful that one's own decision and human action are not sufficient to set one free from them.

This makes it clear that if the language of faith is rightly used, it draws to the full on the experience of the world. For it can carry out its function of binding and loosing only by telling exactly what it is which binds and loosens, and the basis on which one can speak of being bound or loosed. This reference to the concrete situation which is the backing of the language of faith, and absorbs it into itself, is the only thing that makes it possible to impart the experience of freedom. For only when the law is experienced in concrete terms is the gospel experienced.

c. The Challenge to Understanding – Concealment and Revelation – the Experience of the Freedom of Faith

From the point of view of the *challenge to understanding* a theological theory of language has the task of taking into account the fact that the experience of freedom which it claims to offer is the *experience of the freedom of faith*. Here the question is, what attribution of understanding is necessary for the sake of the attribution of faith. A careful distinction has to be made between understanding and faith, in order neither to isolate the one from the other nor to confuse them with each other. And the double sense of attribution, that something is imputed to someone and is also required of them, must be taken into account.

The depth of our crisis of language is such that at the present day the task we have outlined inevitably comes to a head in the problem of how we can speak about God. In this situation it is very serious that the question of God should become isolated and reduced to the dry-as-dust question of the meaning of the word God. And it would be just as wrong, and indeed senseless, for the problem of the way we speak of God to slip over into becoming the question of the propriety of what men say about God. And it is worse still if the answer to this question is tied to a conceptual structure in which God becomes a kind of thing, and the verification of what is said about God is carried out by a kind of process of measurement.

The challenge to understanding made when someone speaks of God does not become clear until it is located in the single vast context of the knowledge of God, the knowledge of oneself, and the knowledge of the world. Then the aspect of experience is not applied to faith as it were as an afterthought. Rather, it becomes clear that faith cannot be interpreted otherwise than in relation to experience, including Luther's *contra omnem experientiam*.

When we return again to consider the structure of polarity in the language of faith, we encounter here the relationship between *concealment and revelation*. By contrast to the legalist understanding which isolates one from the other, so that the relationship between concealment and revelation is turned into a consecutive one, the relationship which is in accordance with the gospel is one in which each coexists with the other and is within the other. The revelation of God is a revelation in concealment, and indeed in a concealment under its contrary, *absconditas sub contrario*. Consequently, theology cannot be a *theologia gloriae*, but must be a *theologia crucis*, that is, if it is to persevere in the attribution of understanding which is in accordance with the language of faith.

d. Mutual Understanding – Conflict and Peace – the Experience of the Freedom of Faith Leading to Love

With regard to the aim of everything that takes place in language, namely the achievement of mutual understanding, a theological theory of language faces a wide range of tasks. Unfortunately it appears as though it is least of all in matters of theology that language is used and is suitable for obtaining mutual agreement. The *rabies theologorum* and the narrow-mindedness of a good many lay theologians form a disturbing contrast to a theological theory of language which is ultimately intended to lead to the *experience of the freedom of faith* helping people *to exercise love*.

We could mention here, however, not only the many illegitimate reasons, but also the many justifiable ones why theology presents so many examples of insuperable difficulties in achieving mutual agreement and irreconcilable disagreement. In terms of the structure of polarity of the language of faith, the tension between *conflict and peace* arises from issues on a scale which is far more serious than all other problems. Here a truth is at stake for which one must be ready to commit one's very life, since it concerns life itself. And it is this that leaves its mark on the problem of achieving mutual agreement in matters of theology. Just as the language of faith itself is a language of struggle, so theology is, for good reasons, a theory of struggle. But there must be a constant awareness that it is a struggle for the achievement of mutual agreement, and a commitment to a mutual agreement, the necessity and promise of which is based upon the figure of Jesus. The language of faith is only moving in the direction of peace in so far as it takes seriously its origin in the gift of the one peace which is beyond human understanding.

Thus from the point of view of the achievement of mutual agreement, a theological theory of language cannot merely discuss the use of the language of faith in preaching to the world, but must also, and perhaps in the first instance, deal with the use of the language of faith in prayer to God. And just as it is necessary not to get entangled in the detailed problems in the foreground of the use of language, but to direct a theological theory of language to the problems of fundamental theology, so it is essential to go on from there to tackle the many individual problems both of the language of preaching and the language of prayer.

These are among the multitude of tasks to which a mere introduction to a theological theory of language must draw attention, and give some guidance to the way they can properly be evaluated and tackled. But it must be left to those who have the calling and talent to deal with them, as well as with the basic problems we have barely sketched.

Epilogue, as a Guide

Let us return now to the starting point of our argument. We perceived the crisis of Christianity as a crisis of language, closely linked to the general crisis of education in our age, which likewise takes the form of a crisis of language. Something would have been achieved if our examination of the problem enabled us to make a more sober and objective judgment of it and to take to heart the responsibility we share for the seriousness of the situation. But we propose in addition three phrases, as a summary of the guidance and encouragement that can be offered. There must be a concern for Christianity come of age, for humane culture and for a well-grounded faith. Let us briefly comment upon and explain these phrases.

I. CHRISTIANITY COME OF AGE

The expression 'maturity' or 'coming of age' has found its adherents in theology at the present day largely in the term 'world come of age'. Its implication is that people in the present age have become mature enough to exercise independent responsibility, even in matters of faith, and should be taken seriously as people emancipated from tutelage. This means no less than that theology should take seriously the Enlightenment, which Kant described as 'man's release from his self-incurred tutelage'.[75] Looking back on the history of the last two centuries, and also bearing in mind the present situation of the world, one may well wonder how mature this world really is. The struggle for emancipation is not in itself a proof of maturity. And the indisputable manifestations of partial maturity ought not to make us overlook the fact that the question of true maturity has to be argued out at a more profound level than that of mere external dependence or independence. This is not to dismiss as unimportant the task with which Christianity is faced in this respect. On the contrary! If Luther's elementary definition of what it is to be a Christian is correct, that is, that a Christian is a free lord over all things and subject to no one, and that at the same time – by virtue of this very freedom! – he is a servant of all things and subject to everyone,[76] this maturity is not something secondary and additional to being a Christian. Rather, faith is true maturity, because it is true freedom. However, when we explicitly use 'mature Christianity' as a slogan, it is intended to draw the attention to the obligation of Christianity in matters of maturity to the 'world come of age' of the present day. What we are going on to say by way of explanation must not be taken as referring to a fully-grown tree with spreading branches, but merely to the seed, the first unobtrusive beginning, on which, however, depends the proper development of the ability to carry out striking and world-shaking tasks. In the first instance, then, if Christianity is to show itself at the present day to be a mature Christianity, then Christians must be prepared to go to some trouble to acquire the necessary information about the faith. Without the least prejudice to the call to Christian action, which is always necessary, the time is ripe to guide Christians to reconsider their faith, and to make available to them the assistance with language which will enable them to say simply and accurately what the Christian faith is and what it has to say. On this depends whether they develop the power of judgment which is appropriate to faith: a power of judgment not merely in Christian matters, but with regard to everything which is put abroad in the form of theories about man, his actions and activities, his loves and sufferings, his life and death.

Thus mature Christianity has something to do with true and pure doctrine. Anyone who has followed the argument so far will hardly suppose that this is merely a statement of unthinking traditionalism. True and pure doctrine is an enormous task which Christianity at the present day has to face, precisely on account of the burning tasks of what we call practical action.

2. HUMANE CULTURE

In a world in which people are more and more learning to measure and control by technical means not only nature but man himself and his social circumstances, we must be concerned that man should not be reduced to a mass-produced product, a cog in a machine. Now more than ever his culture must be humane, and accordingly the circumstances which determine his life must become more human in form. Here again, let us not begin at the end, with the easy search for sensation and headlines. Let us instead consider the essence of a humane culture. Three concrete points are worth making, and they will also make clear something of the specific contribution of Christianity to a liberal education. First of all, a true humane culture must be concerned with historical tradition. This does not mean remaining uncritically within the narrow confines of a single tradition - how fortunate the historical symbiosis between the biblical tradition and that of ancient Greece and Rome has been for Christianity! Neither does it mean being overburdened, in historicist fashion, with historical reminiscences whose relationship to life has either disappeared or has even been arbitrarily removed. Rather, what we mean is an openness to experiences which go beyond the present time and place, and which, as remembered experiences, make one's own time and place broader, deeper, richer and more beautiful, weightier and more serious. Secondly, a true humane culture includes something which is the fruit of a study of history, and not the least of its fruits. This is the ability to compare, to distinguish, to differentiate and to appreciate subtleties, and so to approach what is unfamiliar with a willingness to understand and to do justice even to what presents difficulties. Finally, true humane culture includes what we can describe, adapting Albert Schweitzer's well-known saying about reverence for life, as reverence for language: a conscientious, careful and loving use of words, in the knowledge of what we can destroy with a single word and how much good we can do and how much help we can give with a single word. Consequently it is the concern of a humane culture to resist the abuse of language as an instrument of force and its restriction to nothing more than technical information. It must strive for a language which is worthy of men.

3. WELL-GROUNDED FAITH

This third phrase points to the common source both of mature Christianity and of humane culture. The phrase 'well-grounded faith' seems to unite what is irreconcilable. Faith, we are told, cannot be based upon reason. It believes in the face of reason and experience; it is obedience to an authority which cannot be questioned. Of course there is something quite true in such statements. And as soon as we define more closely what is true in them, we are faced with points of view which take away from these statements the distorting appearance they give of doing violence to humanity. Faith is in flat opposition to superstition. Consequently it demands and encourages the use of reason, and even in matters of faith strives itself for understanding, for an assent to the language of faith which is based on conviction. Understood in this sense, it is the most fundamental way of practising life, and is therefore related in every particular to experience. Even when it is necessary to believe against all experience, this represents a way of accepting and going through life which is pre-eminently related to experience. The overcoming of the crisis in which Christianity finds itself depends essentially upon the realization of the fundamental relationship of faith to life and therefore to experience. This includes the willingness and the courage to concentrate on and restrict ourselves to what we have learned about the necessity of faith in life. Perhaps Christianity must first become very poor in order to rediscover the riches entrusted to it. Perhaps we have to give up a good deal to gain what really matters. But if ever faith is nourished by its foundation, by Jesus Christ himself, it lives by the power of God's love for man and gives way to this power. And where love flourishes, there man flourishes, there the true education of man flourishes and there too human relationships become more human.

Notes

1. I Peter 3 : 15.
2. K. Marx, *Capital*, E.T. by S. Moore and E. Aveling, Vol. I, pt. III, ch. VII (Swan Sonnenschein, London, 12 ed., 1908), p. 156.
3. *Summa Theologica* I, q. 1, ad 4.
4. Weimar Edition, *Table Talk*, 1; 72, 16-24 no. 153. 302, 30-303,3 no. 644.
5. Aquinas, *Summa Theologica* I, q. 1, ad 7.
6. Weimar Edition 40, 2; 328, 1 f.: '. . . *ut proprie sit subiectum Theologiae homo reus et perditus et deus iustificans vel salvator.*' See also my article 'Cognitio Dei et hominis' in *Geist und Geschichte der Reformation, Festgabe H. Rückert zum 65 Geburtstag*, ed. H. Liebing, K. Scholder, K. Aland and W. Eltester, AKG 38, 1966, pp. 271-322, esp. pp. 315ff. Now reprinted in my *Lutherstudien* I, pp. 221-72, esp. pp. 265ff.
7. *Schleiermachers Sendschreiben über seine Glaubenslehre an Lücke*, ed. H. Mulert (1908), 34.
8. *Kurze Darstellung des theologischen Studiums* (1st ed., 1811), § 31. Critical ed. by H. Scholz (1935), p. 10.
9. *Der christliche Glaube* (2nd ed., 1830), § 11. Ed. M. Redeker (1960), I, 74, 29f. E.T. by H. R. Mackintosh, J. S. Stewart, *The Christian Faith* (T. & T. Clark, Edinburgh, 2nd ed., 1960), p. 52.
10. Second *Sendschreiben* to Lücke (see above, n. 7), 35ff.
11. *Der christliche Glaube* (see above, n. 9), introductory sentence to § 9 I, 59, 1-6; E.T., p. 42.
12. Ibid., § 9, 1 I, 61, 21f.; E.T., p. 42.
13. Ibid., § 9, 2 I, 63, 1-16; E.T., p. 43.
14. Second *Sendschreiben* to Lücke (see above, n. 7), 34.
15. See my article 'Profanität und Geheimnis', in G. Ebeling, *Wort und Glaube*, II, *Beiträge zur Fundamentaltheologie und zur Lehre von Gott* (1969), pp. 184-208.

16. G. W. F. Hegel, *Grundlinien der Philosophie des Rechts*, ed. H. Glockner, 7, 35; E.T. by T. M. Knox, *Philosophy of Right* (Oxford University Press, London, 1942), pp. 11, 12f.

17. Ibid., pp. 36f.; E.T., pp. 12f.

18. K. Marx, *Die Frühschriften*, ed. S. Landshut (1968), p. 341; E.T. by T. B. Bottomore and M. Rubel, *Karl Marx; Selected Writings in Sociology and Social Philosophy* (C. A. Watts, London, 1956), p. 69.

19. G. W. F. Hegel, *Vorlesungen über die Geschichte der Philosophie*, ed. H. Glockner, 17, 86.

20. §§ 113-63.

21. D. Bonhoeffer, *Widerstand und Ergebung* (1951), pp. 206f; E.T., *Letters and Papers from Prison* (SCM Press, London, and Macmillan, New York, 3rd ed., 1971), p. 300.

22. Ibid., pp. 261f.; E.T., pp. 382-3. For similar ideas in modern Christian writers, cf. H. Blanke, *Das Menschenbild in der modernen Literatur als Frage an die Kirche* (1966), pp. 35ff. A characteristic statement quoted there is: 'It would therefore perhaps be much better to keep silence . . . There has already been far too much talking and chattering. The present world situation demands, in the Christian realm first of all, something different. I recall a remark by Edzard Schaper in his book *Die letzte Welt*: "There is probably only one convincing theology left, and that is the theology of martyrdom, or shall we say of personal example: there has been enough thinking and talking." ' (W. Schmied, in *Gibt es heute christliche Dichtung?* (1960), pp. 75f.)

23. Op. cit., p. 207; E.T., p. 300.

24. The text from which the quotation is made in the German is in Hugo von Hofmannsthal, *Gesammelte Werke in Einzelausgaben, Prosa II* (1951), pp. 7-22.

25. Ibid., p. 12.

26. Ibid., p. 13.

27. Ibid., pp. 13f.

28. Ibid., p. 12.

29. Ibid., p. 14.

30. Ibid., p. 15.

31. Ibid., p. 16.

32. Ibid., p. 17.

33. Ibid., p. 18.
34. Ibid., p. 20.
35. Ibid., p. 17.
36. Ibid., pp. 18f.
37. Ibid., p. 21.
38. Ibid., p. 22.
39. Isaiah 28 : 19, according to Luther's translation (RSV: 'It will be sheer terror to understand the message').
40. Matthew 12 : 34.
41. Quoted in H. Mayer, *Das Geschehen und das Schweigen. Aspekte der Literatur*. Edition Suhrkamp 342 (1969), p. 66.
42. Weimar Edition 3; 255, 37.
43. *Über den Humanismus* (1946), Klostermann edition (Frankfurt, 1947), p. 5. The phrase is found often in Heidegger.
44. James 3 : 9f.
45. James 3 : 2-4.
46. James 3 : 5f.
47. James 3 : 7f.
48. Job 2 : 11-13.
49. John 8 : 1-11.
50. Weimar Edition 6; 404, 11f.
51. Weimar Edition 4; 365, 5-14.
52. '*Leibhafte Grammatik*': E. Rosenstock-Huessy, *Die Sprache des Menschengeschlechts. Eine leibhafte Grammatik in vier Teilen* I (pts. 1 and 2) (1963); II (pts. 3 and 4) (1964). Cf. I, pp. 354ff.
53. Weimar Edition 39, 2; 104, 24: '*Spiritus sanctus habet suam grammaticam.*' This statement is made with reference to the question whether the grammatically admissible transformation of the statement that Christ's human nature is created into the statement '*Christus est creatura*' is also theologically admissible.
54. Weimar Edition 39, 2; 303, 22-304, 1 (concerning the doctrine of the Trinity): '*Oportet hic etiam grammaticam totam induere novas voces, cum loqui vult de Deo. Cessat etiam numeri ordo: unus, duo, tres. In creaturis quidem valet, sed hic nullus numeri ordo, loci et temporis est. Drumb muss mans hie gar anderst machen et constituere aliam formam loquendi, quam est illa naturalis.*'
55. Weimar Edition 5; 27, 8: '*Primo grammatica videamus, verum ea theologica.*'

56. In the exposition of the eighth (ninth) commandment in the *Shorter Catechism*, Weimar Edition 30, 1; 288, 15-17.

57. Weimar Edition 5; 159, 9-12: '. . . *ut sit verissimum proverbium: Mundus regitur opinionibus, et tales cuique res, qualis opinio rerum, contemptae nulli neque nocent, neque prosunt, aestimatae autem tum prosunt, tum nocent.*' ('. . . so that the proverb is very true, that the world is governed by opinions, and to everyone things are as they seem to him; if they are despised, they neither harm anyone nor are of use to anyone; but if they are highly thought of, they are sometimes of use, and sometimes harmful.')

58. Isidorus Hispalensis, *Etymologiae sive origines* II, 1, 1 (Scriptorum classicorum bibliotheca Oxoniensis, ed. W. M. Lindsay, 1911): '*Rhethorica est bene dicendi scientia in civilibus quaestionibus, [eloquentia copia] ad persuadendum iusta et bona.*' Cf. also H. Lausberg, *Handbuch der literarischen Rhetorik* (1960), § 33.

59. M. F. Quintilian, *Institutiones oratoriae* III, 5, 1 (ed. L. Radermacher, Teubner, 1907): '*Omnis autem oratio constat aut ex iis quae significantur, aut ex iis quae significant, id est rebus et verbis.*' Cf. also Lausberg, op. cit., § 45.

60. Lausberg, op. cit., § 453.

61. M. T. Cicero, *De oratore* 3, 125 (ed. K. F. Kvmaniecki, Teubner, 1969): '*rerum enim copia verborum copiam gignit; et, si est honestas in rebus ipsis, de quibus dicitur, existit ex re naturalis quidam splendor in verbis . . . ita facile in rerum abundantia ad orationis ornamenta sine duce, natura ipsa, si modo est exercitata, delabitur.*' ('For riches in the knowledge of the subject produces a fullness of words; and if there is moral value in the things themselves, which are being spoken of, the content itself brings a certain natural splendour in the words . . . so anyone who has to write or speak can pass easily, without guidance, by nature itself, if only he is exercised enough, from the fullness of matter to the adornments of the speech.')

62. Ibid., 1, 142: '*cumque esset omnis oratoris vis ac facultas in quinque partes distributa, ut deberet reperire primum quid diceret, deinde inventa non solum ordine, sed etiam momento quodam atque iudicio dispensare atque componere; tum ea denique vestire atque ornare oratione; post memoria saepire; ad extremum agere cum dignitate et venustate . . .*' ('And since the influence and skill of every

orator can be divided into five parts, first, that he must first find what he is to say; then set out and put together what he has worked out not only in proper order, but with a certain power of conviction and good judgment; then clothe and adorn it with language; then commit it to memory; and finally come forward with dignity and grace . . .')

63. K. Marx, *Capital*, Preface to 2nd German edition, trans. Moore and Aveling, p. XXX: 'The mystification which dialectic suffers in Hegel's hands by no means prevents him from being the first to present the general form of working in a comprehensive and conscious manner. With him it is standing on its head. It must be turned right side up again, if you would discover the rational kernel within the mystical shell.'

64. *Zeitschrift für Theologie und Kirche* 63 (1966), pp. 49-87.

65. H. Albert, *Traktat über kritische Vernunft* (1968), p. 143.

66. Ibid., p. 144.

67. Ibid., p. 149.

68. *Philosophische Rundschau* 16 (1969), p. 283.

69. B. L. Whorf, *Language, Thought and Reality* (Chapman & Hall, London, and John Wiley & Sons, New York, 1956), p. 212.

70. See also p. 100 above.

71. Psalm 116: 11 (AV). Romans 3 : 4: '*Est autem Deus verax, omnis autem homo mendax.*'

72. See also p. 153 above.

73. Genesis 4 : 1.

74. John 3 : 21; 1 John 1 : 6.

75. I. Kant, *Beantwortung der Frage: Was ist Aufklärung?* in *Werke*, ed. W. Weischedel, VI, p. 53; E.T. by Lewis White Beck, 'What is Enlightenment?' in *Foundations of the Metaphysics of Morals* (Bobbs-Merrill, Indianapolis, 1959), p. 85.

76. Weimar Edition 7; 21, 1-4.

Acknowledgments

The Scripture quotations in this publication are from the Revised Standard Version Bible, copyright 1946, 1952 and © 1971, by the Division of Christian Education, National Council of the Churches of Christ in the U.S.A., and are used by permission. The translator and publishers also wish to acknowledge their indebtedness for permission to reproduce copyright material from the following books: *Letters and Papers from Prison* by Dietrich Bonhoeffer, enlarged edition, copyright © 1953, 1967, 1971 by SCM Press Ltd., reprinted with permission of The Macmillan Company, New York, and SCM Press, London; *Philosophy of Right* by G. W. F. Hegel, translated by T. M. Knox, and reprinted by permission of The Clarendon Press, Oxford; *The Christian Faith* by Friedrich Schleiermacher, translated by H. R. Mackintosh and J. S. Stewart, and published by T. & T. Clark, Edinburgh.